Cutting
and Self-Harm

Psychological Disorders

Psychological Disorders

Cutting and Self-Harm

Heather Barnett Veague, Ph.D.

Series Editor
Christine Collins, Ph.D.
Research Assistant Professor of Psychology
Vanderbilt University

Foreword by
Pat Levitt, Ph.D.
Director, Vanderbilt Kennedy Center
for Research on Human Development

CHELSEA HOUSE
PUBLISHERS
An imprint of Infobase Publishing

Cutting and Self-Harm

Chelsea House
An imprint of Infobase Publishing
132 West 31st Street
New York NY 10001

Library of Congress Cataloging-in-Publication Data
Veague, Heather Barnett.
  Cutting and self-harm / Heather Barnett Veague ; consulting editor, Christine
Collins ; foreword by Pat Levitt.
      p. cm. — (Psychological disorders)
  Includes bibliographical references and index.
  ISBN-13: 978-0-7910-9003-9 (alk. paper)
  ISBN-10: 0-7910-9003-5 (alk. paper)
  1. Self-injurious behavior. 2. Self-mutilation. I. Collins, Christine E. (Christine
Elaine) II. Title. III. Series.
  RC569.5.S48V42 2008
  616.85'82—dc22   2008000519

Chelsea House books are available at special discounts when purchased in
bulk quantities for businesses, associations, institutions, or sales promotions.
Please call our Special Sales Department in New York at (212) 967-8800 or
(800) 322-8755.

You can find Chelsea House on the World Wide Web at http://www.chelseahouse.com

Text design by Keith Trego
Cover design by Keith Trego and Ben Peterson

Printed in the United States of America

Bang EJB 10 9 8 7 6 5 4 3 2 1

This book is printed on acid-free paper.

All links and Web addresses were checked and verified to be correct at the time of
publication. Because of the dynamic nature of the Web, some addresses and links
may have changed since publication and may no longer be valid.

Table of Contents

Foreword

Pat Levitt, Ph.D.
Vanderbilt Kennedy
Center for Research
on Human Development

Think of the most complicated aspect of our universe, and then multiply that by infinity! Even the most enthusiastic of mathematicians and physicists acknowledge that the brain is by far the most challenging entity to understand. By design, the human brain is made up of billions of cells called neurons, which use chemical neurotransmitters to communicate with each other through connections called synapses. Each brain cell has about 2,000 synapses. Connections between neurons are not formed in a random fashion, but rather are organized into a type of architecture that is far more complex than any of today's supercomputers. And, not only is the brain's connective architecture more complex than any computer; its connections are capable of *changing* to improve the way a circuit functions. For example, the way we learn new information involves changes in circuits that actually improve performance. Yet some change can also result in a disruption of connections, like changes that occur in disorders such as drug addiction, depression, schizophrenia, and epilepsy, or even changes that can increase a person's risk of suicide.

Genes and the environment are powerful forces in building the brain during development and ensuring normal brain functioning, but they can also be the root causes of psychological and neurological disorders when things go awry. The way in which brain architecture is built before birth and in childhood will determine how well the brain functions when we are adults, and even how susceptible we are to such diseases as depression, anxiety, or attention disorders, which can severely disturb brain function. In a sense, then, understanding how the brain is built can lead us to a clearer picture of the ways in which our brain works, how we can improve its functioning, and what we can do to repair it when diseases strike.

Brain architecture reflects the highly specialized jobs that are performed by human beings, such as seeing, hearing, feeling, smelling, and moving. Different brain areas are specialized to control specific functions. Each specialized area must communicate well with other areas for the brain to accomplish even more complex tasks, like controlling body physiology—our patterns of sleep, for example, or even our eating habits, both of which can become disrupted if brain development or function is disturbed in some way. The brain controls our feelings, fears, and emotions; our ability to learn and store new information; and how well we recall old information. The brain does all this, and more, by building, during development, the circuits that control these functions, much like a hard-wired computer. Even small abnormalities that occur during early brain development through gene mutations, viral infection, or fetal exposure to alcohol can increase the risk of developing a wide range of psychological disorders later in life.

Those who study the relationship between brain architecture and function, and the diseases that affect this bond, are neuroscientists. Those who study and treat the disorders that are caused by changes in brain architecture and chemistry are psychiatrists and psychologists. Over the last 50 years, we have learned quite a lot about how brain architecture and chemistry work and how genetics contributes to brain structure and function. Genes are very important in controlling the initial phases of building the brain. In fact, almost every gene in the human genome is needed to build the brain. This process of brain development actually starts prior to birth, with almost all the neurons we will ever have in our brain produced by mid-gestation. The assembly of the architecture, in the form of intricate circuits, begins by this time, and by birth we have the basic organization laid out. But the work is not yet complete because billions of connections form over a remarkably long period of time, extending through puberty. The brain of a child is being built and modified on a daily basis, even during sleep.

While there are thousands of chemical building blocks, such as proteins, lipids, and carbohydrates, that are used much like bricks and mortar to put the architecture together, the highly detailed connectivity that emerges during childhood depends greatly upon experiences and our environment. In building a house, we use specific blueprints to assemble the basic structures, like a foundation, walls, floors, and ceilings. The brain is assembled similarly. Plumbing and electricity, like the basic circuitry of the brain, are put in place early in the building process. But for all of this early work, there is another very important phase of development, which is termed experience-dependent development. During the first three years of life, our brains actually form far more connections than we will ever need, almost 40 percent more! Why would this occur? Well, in fact, the early circuits form in this way so that we can use experience to mold our brain architecture to best suit the functions that we are likely to need for the rest of our lives

Experience is not just important for the circuits that control our senses. A young child who experiences toxic stress, like physical abuse, will have his or her brain architecture changed in regions that will result in poorer control of emotions and feelings as an adult. Experience is powerful. When we repeatedly practice on the piano or shoot a basketball hundreds of times daily, we are using experience to model our brain connections to function at their finest. Some will achieve better results than others, perhaps because the initial phases of circuit-building provided a better base, just like the architecture of houses may differ in terms of their functionality. We are working to understand the brain structure and function that result from the powerful combination of genes building the initial architecture and a child's experience adding the all-important detailed touches. We also know that, like an old home, the architecture can break down. The aging process can be particularly hard on the ability of brain circuits to function at their best because positive change comes less readily as we get older. Synapses may be lost and brain chemistry can change over time. The difficulties in understanding how architecture gets built are paralleled by the complexities of what happens to that architecture as we grow older. Dementia associated with brain deterioration as a complication of Alzheimer's disease and memory loss associated with aging or alcoholism are active avenues of research in the neuroscience community.

There is truth, both for development and in aging, in the old adage "use it or lose it." Neuroscientists are pursuing the idea that brain architecture and chemistry can be modified well beyond childhood. If we understand the mechanisms that make it easy for a young, healthy brain to learn or repair itself following an accident, perhaps we can use those same tools to optimize the functioning of aging brains. We already know many ways in which we can improve the functioning of the aging or injured brain. For example, for an individual who has suffered a stroke that has caused structural damage to brain architecture, physical exercise can be quite powerful in helping to reorganize circuits so that they function better, even in an elderly individual. And you know that when you exercise and sleep regularly, you just feel better. Your brain chemistry and architecture are functioning at their best. Another example of ways we can improve nervous system function are the drugs that are used to treat mental illnesses. These drugs are designed to change brain chemistry so that the neurotransmitters used for communication between brain cells can function more normally. These same types of drugs, however, when taken in excess or abused, can actually damage brain chemistry and change brain architecture so that it functions more poorly.

As you read the Psychological Disorders series, the images of altered brain organization and chemistry will come to mind in thinking about complex diseases such as schizophrenia or drug addiction. There is nothing more fascinating and important to understand for the well-being of humans. But also keep in mind that as neuroscientists, we are on a mission to comprehend human nature, the way we perceive the world, how we recognize color, why we smile when thinking about the Thanksgiving turkey, the emotion of experiencing our first kiss, or how we can remember the winner of the 1953 World Series. If you are interested in people, and the world in which we live, you are a neuroscientist, too.

Pat Levitt, Ph.D.
Director, Vanderbilt Kennedy Center
for Research on Human Development
Vanderbilt University
Nashville, Tennessee

What Is Self-Harm?

Although unpleasant, physical pain serves a purpose. When the body hurts, it means that something is wrong. This message is a signal to change behavior. For example, if someone grabs the handle of a pan on the stove and it burns, they will quickly pull their hand away. The speed with which someone pulls his hand away serves as protection; to continue to hold the pan can cause a serious burn. For all the effort most of us make to avoid pain, it is difficult to imagine that some people hurt themselves intentionally. People who hurt themselves on purpose are engaging in **self-harm**, or self-injurious behaviors.

One form of self-harm is **cutting**. Someone who cuts himself uses a sharp object to break the skin or to draw blood. Other self-harmers might burn themselves by putting out a lit cigarette on their skin or bruising themselves. These behaviors are rare, and yet they are of significant concern. Although usually nonlethal, self-harming behaviors do carry a risk of serious injury. More importantly, they usually signal a greater problem—emotional or psychological distress. Sometimes they are a marker of undiagnosed mental illness, one that requires medication, therapy, or hospitalization. Any form of self-harm is a call for help and should be taken seriously.

> **CASE STUDY**
>
> Amanda is a 14-year-old honors student in the ninth grade. She has many friends and is well liked by teachers and her

1

peers. Amanda loves to play the piano, run cross-country, and is an excellent ballet dancer. To all who know her, Amanda lives a nearly perfect life.

Until last summer, Amanda considered herself pretty lucky. She loved her parents and even got along with her little brother Matt. Then, right after the family vacation to Hawaii, Amanda's parents told her that they were separating. This came as a real shock to Amanda, who never suspected that her family would break up. Her brother yelled at their father, blaming him for spending too much time at the office. Her mother sat silently, staring at her hands and picking at her nails. Amanda wanted to cry but found that she couldn't—she felt like she was numb and powerless.

Her father moved out the next day. School was just about to start again and Amanda was afraid of telling her friends what had happened over the summer. While Matt was still angry and often took out his anger on his mom, Amanda spent most of her time in her room or at dance class. She didn't think about the divorce very much but just kept trying to keep peace in the house.

One day into the third week of school, Amanda became overwhelmed with shame about her parents' separation. She was tired of feeling numb and alone but didn't know what to do to feel better. While in the shower shaving her legs, she looked at the razor and wondered what it would feel like to drag the blade across the skin on her arm. She cut herself slowly, watching the blood rise up around the blade and then washed it away. She was surprised by how calm it made her feel. She did it again and realized that she felt very little pain. If anything, the sensation of cutting was a relief. Amanda was confused by what she had done and how it made her feel. On the one hand, she was ashamed—she knew her mom would be disappointed and worry about her. On the other hand, she felt powerful and strong.

As the months passed, Amanda's cutting continued. By Christmas, Amanda had begun to cut on the inside of her thighs because it was easier to hide the markings. If someone did notice a wound or scar, Amanda blamed it on her cat, or said that she had nicked herself in the shower. Surprisingly, no one noticed that Amanda seemed to have a lot of scratches and scars. Most people, including her mother, believed that Amanda was dealing with everything very well. She maintained good grades, was excelling at dance, and continued to be helpful at home. For all intents and purposes, Amanda was a model child.

Christmas was a particularly difficult time for Amanda and Matt. Their father announced that he was dating someone new and wanted them to come to his apartment for Christmas dinner. Amanda's mom encouraged them to go, saying that she would spend the holiday with friends. Amanda was upset. Just last year, everyone had been together, and now everything in her life seemed so messed up. In order to help deal with her overwhelming feelings, Amanda got in the shower with her razor. This time, she went too deep and cut into a vein that wouldn't stop bleeding. Amanda passed out and fell through the shower curtain and hit the floor with a thud. Her mother heard the noise, ran into the bathroom, and saw the blood around her daughter. Because her first assumption was that Amanda was seriously ill and had injured herself, she called 9-1-1. The ambulance came and took Amanda to the hospital. Her mother followed in her car and was terrified that something was terribly wrong with her daughter.

Within a few minutes, the attending physician in the emergency room figured out what had happened. She asked everyone to leave and talked to Amanda about what she had done. Although at first Amanda denied it, the doctor helped her to feel safe about admitting her self-harming behaviors. Amanda was assigned a therapist, someone she could talk to about the divorce, her feelings, and the harmful behaviors she had adopted in order to deal with her emotions. Amanda knew that things had gone too far; she knew she needed help learning better strategies of dealing with her feelings. Although she had a long road ahead, Amanda agreed to begin treatment and, with luck, regain control of her life.

TYPES OF SELF-HARM

When self-harm occurs, psychologists need to determine whether or not the behavior is intentional, in an otherwise normal, nonpsychotic individual, or a sign of a more serious type of mental illness like autism or schizophrenia. The type of self-harm described above (cutting by adolescents) is typically understood to be an abnormal behavior but is not necessarily a sign of psychosis or a developmental disorder. The difference between these two groups can be understood by a discussion of the origin of the urge to self-harm. A young girl who cuts herself when feeling stressed or depressed does so by choice and by her own will. She may tell you that she has an uncontrollable impulse to hurt herself, but she understands that the idea comes from her own mind. In this case, this behavior is called **ego-systonic**, meaning the behavior is part of one's self. Alternatively, someone with schizophrenia might cut himself because he hears a voice telling him to do so. In this case, the person believes that the impulse to cut is not his own, but comes from outside his mind. Here, the behavior is called **ego-dystonic**, meaning apart from one's self.

Self-harm falls into four major categories: *major, stereotypic, compulsive,* and *impulsive.* In Chapter 3 there will be a detailed discussion of stereotypic, major, and compulsive **self-injury**. However, for the most part, this text will focus on impulsive self-harm. Impulsive self-harm can also be considered ego-systonic self-harm—self-harm in otherwise normal, healthy individuals.

HISTORY OF SELF-HARM

Self-harming behaviors are not new. People have engaged in self-harm for centuries. There are people in all cultures who engage in self-harm, although the specific behaviors and the explanation for those behaviors may differ. Some religious leaders have encouraged self-harm as a way of purging oneself of sin. **Redemptive suffering**, or the religious belief that human suffering lessens God's punishment, is one explanation for why some religions encourage self-harm. This self-denial usually takes one of two forms: **asceticism** and **corporal mortification** (also called **mortification of the flesh**).

In its most benign form, some religions have encouraged active self-denial, called asceticism, as a way to become closer to God. There is a rich history of asceticism in the history of western civilization. Early Christians were encouraged to deny themselves pleasure, either by fasting or abstaining from alcohol or sexual intercourse. One of the most notable ascetics in the Catholic faith is Saint Catherine of Siena. Saint Catherine (1347–1380) is most celebrated for her extended periods of fasting where she existed on nothing more than the Sacrament, the bread and wine taken as Communion. Indeed, modern asceticism is most often associated with monks, nuns, or priests. Simply taking a vow of poverty or celibacy is a way in which a priest embraces an ascetic lifestyle. Additionally, the Amish, Quakers, and Mennonites all practice asceticism to some

Figure 1.1 Filipino penitents flagellate themselves on Good Friday, 2007. Devotees flagellate themselves as they reenact Jesus's final hours to atone for sins and bring blessings on their families. *AP Photo/Aaron Favila*

degree, by eliminating certain conveniences from their lives in hopes of lessening distraction from more important, spiritual pursuits. Other world religions such as Hinduism, Buddhism, Islam, and Shamanism also endorse ascetic behaviors. However, one need not adhere to a specific religious group or culture to be considered an ascetic. Asceticism is, by definition, simply the practice of self-denial in order to achieve some higher goal. Some warriors have been said to abstain from sex or alcohol before going to battle. A more contemporary example is that of some professional athletes who refrain from certain activities before a big game or competition.

Corporal mortification, or mortification of the flesh, is a more extreme example of self-harm intended to gain spiritual

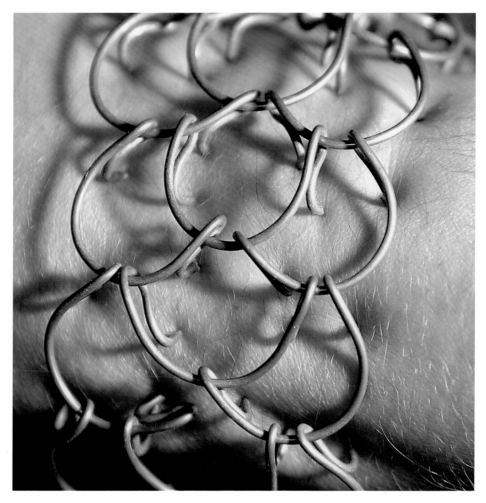

Figure 1.2 Cilice worn by some Opus Dei members. *Orjan F. Ellingvag/Corbis*

or intellectual cleansing. People who engage in corporal mortification typically cut, burn, beat, or whip themselves. In the
middle ages, it was not uncommon to engage in **self-flagellation**,
whipping one's body. In early Christianity and Judaism, some
devout people wore a **cilice**, or a **hairshirt**, an uncomfortable
shirt made of animal hair that was very itchy when worn close
to the skin. Now, the term *cilice* is used for other objects worn

close to the skin under clothes intended to inflict pain. Some members of Opus Dei, a Catholic group founded in Spain in 1928, engage in acts of corporal mortification to aid spiritual healing and growth. Some members of Opus Dei wear a cilice in the form of a spiked chain around the upper thigh that leaves small pricks in the flesh. Others use a discipline, or a whip made of a fabric like macramé, on the back or buttocks. Less extreme measures of self-punishment include sleeping on a board of wood, using wood instead of a pillow, or giving up pleasures like milk or sugar in coffee. These are more regularly used by members of Opus Dei. In the Church of Body Modification, a marginal spiritual organization, extreme measures like body piercing, tattooing, or skin pulling are used in order to obtain spiritual clarity or peace. It is worth noting that because these contemporary groups actively encourage painful behaviors, the groups do not have many members.

In some cultures, painful procedures are used to mark a life stage, major transition, or "coming of age" period. **Genital modification**, like circumcision or clitoridectomy (removal of the clitoris), is used in some African or Australian Aboriginal cultures for young people entering adolescence. Although some of these acts may be voluntary, celebrated within certain cultures, others are forced upon tribe members. As a result, human rights groups like Amnesty International have become involved in a fight against many of these behaviors, viewing them as barbaric and abusive.

SELF-HARM AS MENTAL ILLNESS

The behaviors described above may seem barbaric and out of date. However, taking an historical perspective allows us to appreciate how primal self-harm is. It is not a new phenomenon. Instead, contemporary self-harm is yet another extension of masochistic behaviors that have been used for centuries.

Although the reasons behind the behaviors change, and the behaviors themselves evolve, there just might be some fundamental quality behind all forms of intentional self-harm that is shared. Our current view of self-harm is that it is a sign of mental illness. Understanding when self-harm is a sign of psychopathology requires a general understanding of mental illness.

Defining mental illness is a complicated process. Even in a field as well established as clinical psychology, there remains debate on the most fundamental of questions. What exactly makes one person mentally ill compared to someone else? According to the American Psychiatric Association's *Diagnostic and Statistical Manual of Mental Disorders* (*DSM*), there are three criteria to consider when deciding whether someone has a mental illness. First, there must be some form of *psychological dysfunction*. Psychological dysfunction refers to a breakdown in emotions, thoughts, or behaviors. For example, if Sally has been feeling sad every day, for most of the time, for a month, then her emotions are not functioning properly. Secondly, this dysfunction must cause some distress or impairment in functioning. This seems obvious in Sally's case. She is feeling sad, which is obviously causing her some distress. Maybe Sally is so sad that she can hardly get out of bed to go to work in the

What Is a Mental Disorder?

There are three criteria that define a mental disorder. A person must meet all three of these criteria to be considered to have a mental illness:

1. There is a psychological dysfunction.

2. This dysfunction causes significant distress or impairment.

3. The emotions or behaviors associated with this dysfunction are not typical or expected by one's culture.

morning. Missing work or school is an example of significant impairment in functioning. Lastly, this dysfunction must not be a typical response or one that is culturally expected. If Sally told you that her mother died a month ago and she has been feeling very sad ever since, you might decide that she is having a typical reaction to a traumatic event and, as such, does not have a mental illness. If, however, Sally hasn't experienced a death in her family, you would be more likely to diagnose her with a mental disorder.

Considering what you have just learned about self-harm, how do you decide if someone who engages in it is mentally ill? If we apply the three criteria for mental illness to two different cases, you might be able to see when this behavior is a sign of illness and when it is not.

CASE STUDY: MARTY

Marty is 30 years old and has just joined a new church. To be a member of this church, one is required to walk over hot coals twice a year, on the summer and winter solstices. Before this event, all members meditate together to prepare themselves for the pain they will endure. After walking over the coals, there is a foot washing ceremony followed by a feast and a celebration.

These events happen infrequently and Marty goes to work happily the next day, if a bit sore. Marty tells no one about his church membership, as he knows they won't understand, and will probably think him strange. Still, he finds meaning in these rituals and wouldn't give up his church for anything.

CASE STUDY: ALLISON

Allison is 25 years old and is a paralegal in a small law firm. She is not married, although she has been in several long-term relationships, all of which have been stormy and violent. Whenever a boyfriend threatens to leave her, she becomes frantic and begs him to stay. Sometimes she cuts herself to keep him nearby, even threatening to commit suicide. It is worth noting that Allison has never made a seriously lethal suicide attempt.

Allison cuts herself at least once a month. When she is alone and not dating someone she is less likely to hurt herself. It seems that Allison likes there to be an audience for her self-harm. No one at work knows about Allison's behaviors; after she cuts she always wears long sleeves to the office. However, after she becomes intimate with a boyfriend, she often walks around in tank tops, just to remind him that she can and will hurt herself if necessary.

Marty and Allison are both self-harmers. Marty engages in this behavior less often than Allison, although both limit their behaviors to certain events. If we apply the three criteria to both cases, do either of these people have mental disorders?

1. **Psychological dysfunction.** Marty walks on hot coals twice a year and does so in a controlled environment. Although it seems like a strange choice to want to burn his feet, he engages in it because he believes it will help him obtain spiritual clarity. Marty understands that what he is doing is unorthodox and that most people would think he is crazy. Still, he feels good about himself in general and doesn't see any long-term harm as a result of his behavior. A psychologist could go either way on this first criterion. But because one must meet all three criteria to be diagnosed with a mental disorder, we'll err on the side of caution. For the purposes of illustration we'll argue that

because Marty is hurting himself, a behavior that is irrational and harmful, he does have a psychological dysfunction, specifically one that is behavioral.

Allison, on the other hand, harms herself more frequently. She does this in order to manipulate her boyfriends, specifically to prevent them from leaving her. Allison cannot predict when she will hurt herself; she cuts after she feels threatened and afraid of being alone. She finds she cannot stop herself when she starts and knows that it is irrational and painful. Allison hides her scars from people at work and from her boyfriends until she is comfortable with them. Allison cannot control her self-harming behavior. She uses it for an emotional and manipulative outlet when she feels threatened. This is not a functional way of dealing with the end of a relationship. Thus, we will conclude that Allison has a psychological dysfunction.

2. **Significant distress or impairment.** Marty has no problem with his behavior. He is not worried about it and understands why he walks on hot coals. Marty does not miss work, nor does his personal life suffer in anyway from his behaviors. Marty does not meet this criterion.

Allison is upset about her behavior but does not know how to stop it. Further, cutting herself rarely works in keeping a relationship going. In Allison's case, her behaviors cause her distress (she is upset about cutting) and impairment (they negatively affect her romantic relationships).

3. **Behaviors are not part of a typical response to an event nor are they sanctioned by a culture.** Although we know that Marty does not have a mental illness because he suffers neither distress nor impairment from his fire-walking, we'll apply the third criterion to him for illustrative

purposes. Marty belongs to a church that has been practicing self-harm for hundreds of years. This behavior takes place in a controlled environment and is sanctioned by a large group of peers. Marty's behaviors can be considered to be culturally acceptable. In contrast, Allison does not appear to be having a typical reaction when she cuts herself to keep her boyfriends near. Most people would agree that cutting oneself is not the most productive or effective way to deal with the end of a relationship. Thus, Allison meets all three criteria.

According to these criteria, Marty does not have a mental illness whereas Allison probably does. Although the behaviors are similar in nature, the thoughts and emotions behind them are quite different. Understanding what makes someone engage in self-harm is the first step in determining whether it needs to be treated.

Although psychologists typically agree that many forms of self-harm are indeed signs of mental illness, so far there is no consensus on how best to categorize it. More simply, self-harm does not have a unique diagnosis. There is no diagnosis for someone like Allison that just focuses on her self-harming behaviors. Most psychologists will argue that self-harm does not exist in the absence of other symptoms. Someone who cuts might be evaluated for **borderline personality disorder (BPD)**, a serious form of mental illness in which people can and often do engage in self-harm. Still, self-harm is not a requirement for the diagnosis of BPD. Someone who engages in self-starvation will likely be evaluated for **anorexia nervosa**, but might not meet criteria for the diagnosis because of other factors. These are issues that you will learn about in greater depth later in this text.

(continues on page 16)

Matt Talbot

Until his death, Matt Talbot was considered an ordinary man who lived in ordinary circumstances. Born on May 2, 1856, Matt was the second of 12 children in a poor family in Dublin, Ireland. His father was a heavy drinker, and Matt quit school at age 12 to go to work to help support his family. He took a job with wine merchants and quickly began to sample what they were selling. Taking after his father, Matt soon became a heavy drinker himself. For many years, Talbot was said to have spent every penny on alcohol. As a result, he ran up extensive debts and even stole in order to get his next drink. One day in 1884, at age 28, Talbot spent the day begging his friends for money so that he could continue drinking. No one gave him a penny. That night he went home to his mother and told her he was "taking the pledge," meaning that he was going to start on the path toward sobriety. He went to Cloniffe College, where he pledged to remain sober for three months. After three months, he pledged another six. From that point forward, Talbot abstained from alcohol until his death.

After obtaining his sobriety, Talbot changed his life completely. Being an indifferent Catholic in his youth, Talbot later became pious and devout, spending all of his spare time at mass, in prayer, or in doing good deeds for the church. He went to mass daily, rising at five o'clock in the morning to go before work. While at work he would use his break time to kneel and pray. He read religious works given to him by Dr. Michael Hickey, a professor of philosophy at Cloniffe College.

After his years working for wine merchants, Talbot found a job as a builder. He was a hard worker, always choosing the least desirable and most demanding tasks. Respectful to his bosses and extremely kind to his fellow workers, Talbot was remembered as being willing to stand up for people who were being treated unfairly or unkindly. Although a poor man himself, Talbot was generous and gave away almost everything he had. He began by repaying all of the debts he had accumulated while he was a drinker. Next, he gave to needy friends, or to the Catholic Church, and kept very little for himself. His needs were few, and he gave up all excesses as a sacrifice for his faith.

On June 7th, 1925, Talbot collapsed on his way to mass. He was taken to the hospital, where he died of heart failure. Upon his death, Talbot was undressed and a discovery was made which lifted him from obscurity and brought him to attention in the Catholic Church. Beneath his clothes, Talbot had a chain wound around his waist with more chains around one arm and a leg. Later, his living quarters were inspected. After his mother's death Talbot moved into a tiny apartment with little furniture. All he had was a plank bed with a piece of wood that he used as a pillow.

In the years since his death, Matt Talbot has become a symbol for the recovery movement—those who are addicted to drugs and/or alcohol revere him as a role model for sobriety. Treatment centers for the addicted are named for Matt Talbot around the world. In 1975, Pope Paul XI began the process of canonization for Matthew Talbot, the first step toward sainthood. Whether or not his ascetic lifestyle and self-harming behaviors brought him closer to God, they appear to have made him a hero to many believers.

(continued from page 13)

• • • • • • • •

SUMMARY

Someone who engages in self-harm causes damage to their body. There is evidence of self-harm occurring in various cultures throughout the history of modern civilization. Although a church or religious group may endorse some self-harming behaviors, more and more young people are engaging in self-harm as a way of dealing with complicated emotions. Self-harm is not always a sign of mental illness. In order to determine whether someone is mentally ill, their emotions or behaviors must meet the three criteria specified in this chapter. Even after one concludes that self-harm is a symptom of mental illness, diagnosis is a challenge because there is no specific illness named for self-harmers.

This book will explore many different types of self-harm. You will learn about what causes self-harm and how to treat it. You will read about the biological, psychological, and social foundations of self-harming behavior. Throughout the text you will read case studies illustrating many different situations in which self-harming behavior emerges. Finally, you will learn how a public health approach might be an appropriate means toward eradicating self-harm.

Who Engages in Self-Harm?

Self-harming behaviors are not limited to young women. In fact, people of all ages and from all different backgrounds engage in self-harm. Those who practice self-injurious behavior share certain characteristics, and there are theories that may explain why certain people are more likely to self-injure than others.

CASE STUDY

Richard is a 24-year-old man who dreams of being a professional musician. Two years ago, he graduated from the Berkeley College of Music in Boston, where he trained as a classical guitarist. Since graduation, Richard has been working in the furniture department at a local department store and going to auditions in his spare time. Although he is a talented guitarist, Richard has had little success working as a musician. Competition is fierce, and Richard is beginning to doubt whether he will ever succeed.

Lately, Richard has been feeling depressed. He spends most of his time at work or alone at home with his guitar. He's constantly on edge, waiting for his agent to call him with information about an audition. He keeps his schedule open so that he is generally available. It was a rare occurrence when Richard decided to leave Boston to go home to Rhode Island for the holidays. On this visit, he saw several of his high school friends, all of whom appeared to be very successful.

One was an investment banker in New York and another just graduated from Yale Law School. Both were making generous salaries, whereas Richard's income barely covered his living expenses. He never thought he was one who cared about material things, but being around his old friends made him feel like a failure. His friends asked him about how his music career was coming along. In high school, everyone expected Richard to be a rock star. Richard was ashamed to tell his friends that he was a furniture salesman. He wished he were more successful.

Feeling bad about himself was not new for Richard. When he went away to school, Richard was faced with the realization that he was no longer the big fish in his small high-school pond. Richard was surrounded by brilliant musicians at Berkeley. To help manage his feelings of inadequacy, Richard began abusing alcohol. He gained a reputation for being a risk taker—balancing on high walls and playing with fire. He even played Russian roulette once. In the beginning, Richard only engaged in these behaviors while drinking and while he had an audience. He thought it was exciting and felt invincible. Lately, Richard has been taking more risks in private. When he drinks alone, he sometimes lights matches and burns himself. The pain isn't too bad and he feels strong and capable when he can tolerate it. After a bad day, hurting himself makes him feel more in control.

No one knows about Richard's self-harm. When he's sober, he's embarrassed by what he's done and swears to himself that he won't do it again. However, once he starts drinking again, the urges return. He has heard about girls who cut themselves—he even knew a girl in his dorm who was forced to take a semester off because of her self-harm. Still, it would never occur to Richard to seek psychiatric help for what he's doing—it's not like he's suicidal. In fact, he's just trying to find a way to make his life more tolerable.

DEMOGRAPHICS

Research about self-harm is in its early stages. As a result, there is little consensus about the prevalence, causes, and most effective treatment for self-harming behavior. In fact, researchers and clinicians do not even agree about what to call self-harming behavior. Terms like *self-injury*, **self-mutilation, self-abuse, parasuicide**, *body modification*, and *deliberate self-harm* are all used to describe similar behaviors. Much research is limited to certain types of self-injury, like cutting or mutilating the skin, while other research might focus on self-harm more generally. Self-harming behavior is not considered a mental illness in itself. For these reasons, there are many questions about self-harm left unanswered.

There are very little data about who engages in self-harm and how common it is. People who self-harm typically try to hide their behaviors. Unless they are being treated for psychiatric complaints like depression or anxiety, self-harmers may go unidentified. Indeed, most estimates of the prevalence of self-harm come from people who are receiving treatment for mental illness. As a result, it is difficult to obtain an accurate measure of how prevalent self-harm is in the general population. One of the earliest studies on the prevalence of self-harm was conducted by Karen Conterio and Armando Favazza at the University of Missouri–Columbia. They estimated that approximately 0.75 percent of the population engages in self-injurious behaviors.[1] That means that for every 100 people, there is approximately one person who is a self-harmer. More recent estimates suggest that it is even more common, and about 4 percent of the general adult population has engaged in self-mutilation.[2] You may have

Figure 2.1 Clinical and media reports have suggested that self-harm is on the rise, particularly in adolescent populations. *AP Photo/Lauren Greenfield*

heard that adolescents are at increased risk of practicing self-harm. Indeed, adolescents appear to be more likely than adults to self-injure. In 2003, Shana Ross and Nancy Heath of McGill University reported that approximately 13 percent of Canadian high school students living in urban and suburban areas had performed acts of self-harm.[3]

Clinical and media reports have suggested that self-harm is on the rise, particularly in adolescent populations. A *Los Angeles Daily News* article published in 2004 revealed that the Los Angeles Unified School District was training educators to deal with the dramatic increase in student reports of deliberate self-harm.[4] As a result, researchers have begun to focus on the unique characteristics of self-injury in adolescent populations. In 2001, Philip Boyce, Mark Oakley-Browne, and Simon Hatcher reported a 28 percent increase in adolescents who presented for treatment at a hospital in Oxford, England.[5] Additionally, the Cornell Research Program on Self-Injurious Behavior in Adolescents and Young Adults (http://www.crpsib.com) in Ithaca, New York, reports that college mental health workers agree that self-harming behaviors are indeed on the rise.

What might account for the increase in reports of self-harm? The obvious explanation would be that more people are engaging in these behaviors. The increase in self-harm could be the effect of a **social contagion**: the more people talk about a behavior, the more it gains popularity. Another explanation could be that people are more willing to talk about and seek help for self-harm. Thus, no more people are actually self-injuring; rather, self-harmers are more likely to receive clinical attention. Perhaps the stigma of self-harm has been lifted and those who hurt themselves are more comfortable entering treatment. Alternatively, clinicians may be more aware of the problem of self-harm and thus more likely to ask about and identify self-harmers. Any or all of these explanations may account for the reported rise in self-harming behaviors. Future research will undoubtedly address this issue.

GENDER AND SELF-HARM

Research suggests that women are more likely than men to practice deliberate self-harm. Armando Favazza and Karen Conterio found that 97 percent of their self-harmers were women.[6] Similarly, Shana Ross and Nancy Heath found that 64 percent of their adolescent self-injurers were female.[7] Although most researchers and clinicians agree that women are more likely to practice deliberate self-harm than men, there is no consensus why. Some theorists believe that young girls are taught to **internalize** anger, or direct their anger inward. This would mean that, as children, girls are not encouraged to

Figure 2.2 Research suggests that women are more likely than men to self-harm. *Heide Benser/zefa/Corbis*

express emotions that might upset others. If someone is discouraged from expressing feelings, one way of managing sadness or psychological pain might be to harm oneself in private. According to this same theory, boys are taught to **externalize** their feelings, or direct their anger toward others. As a result, a boy would be more likely to hurt someone else rather than himself.

There is another explanation for why females might appear to engage in self-harm more than males. In the case study earlier in this chapter, Richard knows of other people who hurt themselves, but it never occurrs to him to talk to someone about his problems. Indeed, females are more likely to seek help for mental illness, specifically for depression and anxiety disorders. Because most estimates of the prevalence of self-harm come from treatment settings, females would appear to be more likely to self-harm simply because they are more likely to be found in mental health settings. If this is true, perhaps males are just as likely to engage in self-harm, but much less likely to receive treatment for it.

A final possible explanation for the gender difference in self-harm comes from the idea that there is **gender bias** in the category, or definition, of self-harm. A category is considered to have gender bias if, by definition, it includes traits or behaviors that are more strongly associated with one gender versus another. This is difficult to determine given that, as yet, self-harm is not in itself a category of mental illness. However, because self-harmers are generally assumed to be female, mental health workers might look for signs of self-harm in women but neglect to look for these signs in men. Thus, while there might be no true difference in the prevalence of self-harm in men and women, clinicians would report one.

LONG-TERM CONSEQUENCES OF SELF-HARM

Self-harm is not, by definition, an act of suicide. Death is not an intended consequence of self-injury. Unfortunately, people who hurt themselves can occasionally go too far and die. The

(continues on page 26)

Elizabeth Wurtzel

Elizabeth Wurtzel is a writer most celebrated for the publication of her memoir, *Prozac Nation* (Riverhead Books, 1995). Wurtzel describes an adolescence punctuated by depression, anxiety, drug and alcohol abuse, and self-injury. Teachers described her as an overachiever, and she attended Harvard University as an undergraduate. Her self-injury began in high school and consisted mainly of cutting her arms and legs. In the following passage, she describes her first experience with self-harm: [8]

I felt that I was wrong—my hair was wrong, my face was wrong, my personality was wrong—my God, my choice of flavors at the Häagen Dazs shop after school was wrong! How could I walk around with such pasty white skin, such dark, doleful eyes, such straight anemic hair, such round hips and such a small clinched waist? How could I let anybody see me this way? How could I expose other people to my person, to this bane to the world? I was one big mistake. And so, sitting in the locker room, petrified that I was doomed to spend my life hiding from people this way, I took my keys out of my knapsack. On the chain was a sharp nail clipper, which had a nail file attached to it. I rolled down my knee socks (we were required to wear skirts to school) and looked at my bare white legs. I hadn't really started shaving yet, only from time to time because my mother considered me too young, and I looked at the delicate peach fuzz, still soft and untainted. A perfect, clean canvas. So I took the nail file, found its sharp edge, and ran it across my lower leg, watching a red line of blood appear across my skin. I was surprised at how straight the line was and at how easy it was for me to hurt myself in this way. It was almost fun. I was always the sort to pick scabs and peel sunburned skin in sheets off my shoulders, always pestering my body. This was just the next step. And how much more satisfying it was to muck up my own body than relying on mosquitoes and walks in the country among thorny bushes to do it for me. I made a few more scratches, alternating between legs, this time moving

Figure 2.3 Elizabeth Wurtzel, author of *Prozac Nation. Frank Veronsky / Corbis*

the file more quickly, less cautiously. I did not, you see, want to kill myself. Not at that time, anyway. But I wanted to know that if need be, if the desperation got so terribly bad, I could inflict harm on my body. And I could. Knowing this gave me a sense of peace and power, so I started cutting up my legs all the time. Hiding the scars from my mother became a sport of its own. I collected razor blades, I bought a Swiss Army knife, I became fascinated with different kinds of sharp edges and the different cutting sensations they produced. I tried out different shapes—squares, triangles, pentagons, even an awkwardly carved heart, with a stab wound at its center, wanting to see if it hurt the way a real broken heart could hurt. I was amazed and pleased to find that it didn't.

(continued from page 23)

term *parasuicide* refers to deliberate self-harm that could have, but did not, result in death. It is unclear whether parasuicidal behaviors are intended as suicidal gestures or merely self-injurious. Regardless, all parasuicidal acts should be taken seriously, as people who engage in parasuicidal acts are significantly more likely to eventually die at their own hand.

Self-injurious behavior is similar to drug and alcohol use in that it can become addictive. When a person begins to use drugs or alcohol, they can begin by using small amounts to give them relief from bad feelings or provide a temporary escape from a difficult reality. After using substances for a period of time, one requires more drug or alcohol to attain the same effect. Self-injury may affect the body similarly. After the body is hurt, **endorphins** are released to help relieve pain. Someone who self-harms may need more and more endorphins to get the same kind of "rush" from pain. This would require more and more self-harm, effectively causing more and more damage to the body. When this occurs, suicide can result from an "overdose" of self-injury.[11]

Specific kinds of deliberate self-harm pose unique risks to health and may cause permanent injury. People who cut themselves may accidentally cut too deep and sever a major vein or artery. Burning can cause serious and permanent tissue damage, and untreated burns may become infected. Infection or gangrene may result from people who cut or pick at their wounds. Although extremely rare, some self-harmers poison themselves by ingesting chemicals or cleaning solvents. Intentional poisoning can cause severe illness and permanently damage internal organs.

• • • • • • • •

SUMMARY

Self-harm affects somewhere between 1 and 4 percent of the general population and is much more common in mental-health treatment settings. Although there is some controversy surrounding exactly how gender and self-harm are related, most researchers agree that females are more likely to engage in self-harm than males. Self-harm does appear to be increasing in prevalence, although it is unclear whether more people are indeed engaging in self-harm or are just more willing to talk openly about it. People who hurt themselves are often trying to manage painful and intense emotions and use self-injury as a coping strategy. Although self-harm is not, by definition, intended to result in death, suicide is often an unfortunate consequence. People who practice deliberate self-harm put themselves at risk of serious illness, injury, and death.

3

Self-Harm
and Mental Illness

Self-injury is symptom or sign of several mental disorders.
The prevalence of self-injury in mental-health treatment settings confirms that people who engage in self-harm are often
suffering from major mental illness. Armando Favazza of the
University of Missouri at Columbia has developed a system of
categorizing self-harm as it appears in recognized psychiatric
conditions. According to his system, there are four types of self-
harm: **stereotypic, major, compulsive,** and **impulsive. Stereotypic
self-injurious behaviors** are repetitive, often rhythmic behaviors
and are associated with developmental disorders such as autism
or **Tourette's disorder.** Head banging is the most typical stereotypic self-injurious behavior. People with psychotic disorders,
such as **schizophrenia,** may practice major self-injurious behaviors that cause a great deal of tissue damage like castration or
amputation. Compulsive self-harm, behaviors that occur daily
and are often ritualistic may be present in obsessive-compulsive
disorder and **trichotillomania,** which involves repetitive hair pulling. Finally, impulsive self-harm, such as ego-systonic cutting,
often occurs in people with borderline personality disorder or
an **eating disorder.**[9]

AUTISM: STEREOTYPIC SELF-HARM
One of the most severe and disabling disorders diagnosed in
childhood is **autistic disorder.** The National Institute of Mental

Health reports that approximately 3.4 out of every 1,000 children ages 3 to 10 have autism. Autism is a developmental disorder that involves deficits in language, perceptual, and motor development. Social development is markedly delayed in people with autism and is a typical sign of the disorder that appears when a child seems apart from others, from a very early age. Most children with autism exhibit speech impairment; some rarely speak in order to communicate, instead using words repetitively. Additionally, mental retardation is common in autism. Some children with autism are remarkably skilled at manipulating objects—tasks like assembling puzzles or identifying patterns. However, when puzzles have a social meaning, like telling a story, people with autism have great difficulty.

CASE STUDY: AUTISM

Betsy, a 22-year-old woman diagnosed with autism, has been living in some sort of residential treatment facility since she was four years old. Recently, she has been referred to an inpatient psychiatric hospital because the staff of her group home determined that she needs additional care. Unlike other patients in the group home, Betsy preferred to stay by herself. She interacted with few staff members, all of whom had been there since Betsy arrived. Recently, her self-abuse became more severe. Betsy had been pounding on her legs and biting her hand daily. As a result, her legs are bruised and her hand looks as if it might become infected.

When Betsy arrived at the hospital, she spent much of her time reading a children's book that she discovered in the waiting room. She talks with little emotion, her speech is monotonous, and it is difficult to get her to respond. When the doctor tries to get her to stop reading the book, she responds by pounding on her legs with her fist. She rocks back and forth continually throughout the interview. She makes little eye contact and seems not to notice most other people they encounter. From time to time she repeats a single phrase, "blum blum." When the doctor is able to examine Betsy, he notices severe bruises all over both of her legs.

Betsy's mother had a normal pregnancy, labor, and delivery. Her parents recall that she was an unusually easy baby. When Betsy was unable to speak at age two, her parents became concerned. Her parents initially thought she might be deaf, but this was obviously not the case, as she responded with panic to the sound of a vacuum cleaner. As a young child, Betsy "lived in her own world," had not formed attachments to her parents, responded unusually to certain sounds, and always became extremely upset when there were changes in her environment.

By age four, Betsy was still not speaking. Her parents placed her in a state institution after she was diagnosed with autistic disorder. In the year after her placement, Betsy began speaking. However, she did not use speech for communication; rather, she repeated phrases over and over. She had an unusual ability to memorize and became fascinated with reading, even though she appeared not to comprehend anything she read. She exhibited a variety of repetitive physical behaviors, such as rocking and banging her head, that required increasing intervention by staff members. Betsy had spent most of her life living in institutions. Presently, Betsy needed help in all parts of her life—most importantly protecting her from self-harm.[10]

Characteristics of self-harm are seen in the **self-stimulation** in autism. Repetitive movements like head banging, spinning, rocking, and picking at the skin can be practiced for hours. In the autism case study, Betsy hits her legs repeatedly. She hits herself when her routines or activities are disturbed. Some autistic children can become quite enraged when their self-stimulating activities are interrupted. A significant part of treatment for autism is to limit and control these harmful behaviors. Head banging and skin picking can cause long-term health problems and cannot be allowed.

Autism is a lifelong, chronic condition. In general, treatment is rarely effective. Medications are used sparingly and with questionable efficacy. The most promising treatment, particularly for limiting self-stimulating behavior, is **behavioral therapy.** Ivar Lovaas at the University of California, Los Angeles, is a pioneer in the behavioral treatment of autistic children. His treatment strategy involves intensive, one-on-one sessions that usually take place in the child's home. The sessions continue for several hours each day over many years. The treatment is based on learning principles, namely **reinforcement** and **punishment.** Appropriate, positive social behaviors are positively reinforced, and negative behaviors, such as self-harm, are punished. For example, when a child makes eye contact with his parent he receives a piece of candy. The candy then reinforces the eye contact, increasing the likelihood that it will happen again. Reinforcing positive behaviors seems obvious. But how do you effectively, and humanely, punish self-harm? Autistic children do not value social relationships, so a "time out" would likely prove ineffective. Instead, teachers will use physical means of punishment that are unpleasant to the child. For example, if a child begins to bang their head, a teacher might use a water bottle to gently spray a child. This is not a painful act, but it is unpleasant enough to interrupt the harmful behavior. There is some controversy surrounding the use of some forms of punishment for autistic children (e.g., mild electrical shocks used in some treatment settings), although these methods have been found to be relatively effective.

TOURETTE'S DISORDER: STEREOTYPIC SELF-HARM

People who suffer from Tourette's disorder generally attract a great deal of attention. Someone with Tourette's disorder has **tics**, a stereotyped movement or vocalization that is repeated, sudden, and rapid. The disorder is rare, affecting about 1 in every 2,000 people. Like autism, Tourette's is more likely to affect males than females; approximately three times more males than females have the disorder. Symptoms generally emerge around age seven or before the teen years. Rapid or prolonged eye blinking is usually the first tic to appear, and patients might develop other more complex motor tics like doing deep knee bends or stretches. Vocal tics are what make Tourette's disorder unique. Patients with vocal tics might bark, click, grunt, or use understandable words. **Coprolalia**, a vocal tic involving obscene or profane language, affects between 10 and 30 percent of patients with Tourette's disorder.[11]

Tourette's disorder is also associated with stereotypic self-harm. Some individuals with Tourette's may harm themselves by repeatedly banging their head or picking at the skin. Treatment for Tourette's disorder typically involves a combination of medication and psychotherapy. **Antipsychotic medications** such as haloperidol are generally the most effective at reducing motor tics, including the self-harming behaviors. Behavioral treatments involving teaching relaxation techniques can also help reduce the severity of the symptoms of Tourette's.

CASE STUDY: TOURETTE'S DISORDER

Mark is 10 years old and in the fourth grade. He is at his third elementary school, because his parents are convinced that Mark's problems are due to his environment, rather than his biology. Mark has been diagnosed with attention-deficit/hyperactivity disorder and has been medicated with Ritalin for 18 months. Six months ago, Mark's parents noticed that Mark had an exaggerated eye blink, but attributed this to his medication. Just this month, Mark has started grunting occasionally, usually when he is working on his homework. His grunts are very loud and his parents can hear them even several rooms away. More and more often his grunting occurs during a test at school, or any quiet, independent activity. Mark is self-conscious, and every time he grunts, he hits himself in the head. His teacher is concerned that he is going to hurt himself. He tries to control these outbursts but is finding it more and more difficult.

Mark and his parents go to a psychologist that was recommended to them by his school counselor. The psychologist asks Mark's parents a lot of questions about their mental health history. Mark's mother reveals that she has been treated for obsessive-compulsive disorder for years, and that her brother has Tourette's disorder. Because Tourette's disorder is known to run in families, the psychologist is fairly certain that Mark is experiencing early symptoms of the disorder. His parents are concerned that Mark will not be able to live a normal life. They are willing to try anything to get these tics under control so that Mark does not hurt himself physically or socially.

SCHIZOPHRENIA AND PSYCHOTIC DISORDERS: MAJOR SELF-HARM

Schizophrenia is a serious mental illness usually characterized by the presence of **psychotic symptoms** such as **hallucinations, delusions,** or **disorganized thoughts or behavior.** Hallucinations involve sensory experiences that have no real environmental cause.

Thomas joined the armed services in 1968 and was sent to Vietnam when he was 18 years old. After his first deployment of eight months, Thomas was given a medical discharge. He reported that he was hearing voices and was found using the point of a pen to dig pieces of skin out of his arm.

Thomas was sent to a local Veteran's Administration hospital in his home state of California. His parents hardly recognized him when they first visited him. His appearance was disheveled and dirty, and he was wearing a heavy winter coat on a warm spring day. His arms were bandaged and Thomas was not permitted any sharp or pointed objects as the psychiatric staff worried that he would resume hurting himself. Although he began a medication regimen when he arrived at the hospital, not enough time had passed for it to take effect. His parents were terrified by what Thomas told them.

When Thomas left for Vietnam, he was a nice, quiet boy who had a fairly normal childhood. In high school, Thomas ran track and was in the chess club. He was bright, got good grades, and had a few friends. Although Thomas was not a particularly popular boy, he was not disliked. Although he was quiet, his peers accepted him easily because he was a good athlete and smart. When Thomas joined the military, everyone was a bit surprised. They expected that he would go to a good college and maybe even graduate school. Thomas's father was an air force pilot, and Thomas knew that his dad would be proud if he followed in his footsteps. So a month before graduation, Thomas joined the air force.

Until he left for basic training, Thomas had never been away from his family. Going from his easygoing family into the air force was stressful. He was forced to get up at 5 a.m.

every day and perform strenuous exercise. He was yelled at, forbidden from doing anything without direction by a superior officer, and scolded and humiliated when he couldn't keep up. Thomas found he couldn't sleep at night and was beginning to have anxiety attacks.

On the flight to Saigon, Thomas thought he heard his commanding officer's voice. He was surprised since they were on different planes. The voice got louder and louder and was telling him that he would always know what Thomas was thinking. Thomas was confused, and afraid, and frustrated when he couldn't make the voices stop. After a month of hearing the voice get louder and more critical, Thomas determined that his body was being taken over by his commanding officer. He felt that he couldn't do what he wanted to do—that his every move was orchestrated by someone else. Thomas felt betrayed by his body and wanted to kill whatever was taking him over. He started poking himself with pencils and pens in order to destroy this other person, but it generally gave him little relief. When the other men noticed what he was doing, they reported him and sent Thomas to their unit physician. Within days after this visit, Thomas was sent home and immediately placed in a psychiatric hospital.

Thomas was experiencing auditory hallucinations when he heard his commanding officer talking to him even though he wasn't near. A delusion is a strongly held belief that persists despite evidence to the contrary. Someone with a delusion might believe that aliens are plotting to abduct him. Disorganized thinking is characterized by speech that is extremely difficult to follow. People who have disorganized thinking might change topic with no warning and have difficulty staying on track or answering questions. Finally, people with grossly disorganized behavior may have difficulty maintaining personal hygiene and appear markedly disheveled and disoriented.

Schizophrenia is associated with a high rate of suicide. More than 10 percent of people with schizophrenia eventually commit suicide, and the percentage of those who attempt it is even higher. Because suicidal behavior is so common in schizophrenia, it is often difficult to determine how prevalent nonsuicidal self-injurious behavior is in this population.

Although there is little empirical research investigating self-harm in schizophrenia, many clinicians agree that it is a problem in the population. Some patients eventually practice self-harm as a result of their psychotic thinking. These acts, though rare, can have devastating consequences. For example, if a patient believes that there are bugs living in his ear, he might use scissors to attempt to remove them. Thomas cut at his arm in order to destroy the other person who he believed was living in his body. Some people with schizophrenia have a higher tolerance for pain and as a result may harm themselves unintentionally. Schizophrenia patients with disorganized behavior might dress in summer clothes on a snowy winter day or, like Thomas, wear a winter coat when it is warm outside. Finally, stereotypic self-harming behavior can also occur in schizophrenia. Like in autism, stereotypies in schizophrenia include rocking, banging, or any repetitive physical movement.

OBSESSIVE-COMPULSIVE DISORDER: COMPULSIVE SELF-HARM

Obsessive-compulsive disorder, typically referred to as OCD, is marked by the presence of obsessions, compulsions, or both. **Obsessions** are recurring, persistent thoughts, impulses, or images that intrude into everyday thinking and cause distress or anxiety. Obsessions are not just extreme worries about everyday problems. They are unreasonable thoughts, like worrying that you have run over a small child with your car, even if you haven't left the house. **Compulsions** occur when someone feels the need to repeat physical behaviors such as washing their hands or checking locks on the doors multiple times. Compulsions can also involve mental behaviors, such as counting things or repeating phrases to avoid some unpleasant event. Compulsive behaviors typically occur as a response to an obsession or according to strictly applied rules. Compulsions serve to reduce tension or anxiety or, in the sufferer's belief, prevent something terrible from happening. People with OCD understand that their obsessions and/or compulsions are unreasonable and excessive. These thoughts and behaviors interfere with one's usual, daily routine.

CASE STUDY: OBSESSIVE-COMPULSIVE DISORDER

Michaela is a 28-year-old homemaker with three children. Although she has always considered herself an anxious person, she has never sought professional help for her problems. Recently her worries have become more and more invasive and troubling. She decided that it was time to see a psychiatrist to try to help alleviate some of her anxiety.

After the birth of her youngest child, Emma, Michaela began to have insomnia because she was so worried that her daughter was going to get cancer. The worries began when Emma was about three weeks old. Although Emma was perfectly healthy, Michaela couldn't stop thinking that her breast milk was poisonous. She knew this was an unreasonable thought, but she couldn't get it out of her head. In order to suppress the obsession, she began washing her hands. She decided that she was being contaminated and that by washing her hands multiple times daily she could stop the spread of poisons into her breast milk. Her hand-washing began benignly; she would wash them once every hour. Over time,

Figure 3.1 Compulsive hand-washing, present in some individuals with obsessive-compulsive disorder, is a form of compulsive self-harm that can lead to raw and bleeding hands and cuticles. *Tomas Bercic/iStockphoto*

her anxiety increased such that she needed to wash her hands more and more to stop the poison obsessions. Now she has a ritual surrounding hand-washing. She begins each hour, on the hour. Her first step is to clean under her nails with a razor blade. Then she wipes her hands with a disposable disinfecting wipe and throws it in the trash. Next, she uses three pumps of liquid soap and lathers up for 5 minutes. Finally, she rinses her hands in scalding hot water and dries them on a paper towel. Before she leaves the sink she pumps three pumps of antibacterial gel into her hands and lets them air dry. The entire hand-washing process takes about 10 minutes each hour. No matter what she is doing, she must stop her activities each day just before the clock strikes the hour so that she can begin her ritual.

Michaela's hands are red and raw from all the hand-washing. Her skin is dried and chapped, and her cuticles are often bleeding. Michaela finds herself picking at her cuticles and pulling the skin off because she is convinced that her nail beds are home to bacteria and poisons. She used to bite her nails but now she would never put her hands near her mouth. Instead she keeps her nails clipped extremely short, often so short that they bleed. She tries to hide her hands from others, including her husband. She knows that her behaviors are unreasonable, but they are the only way to alleviate her anxiety about harming her own children.

Michaela meets diagnostic criteria for obsessive-compulsive disorder. Her daily life is profoundly affected by her intrusive thoughts and compensatory behaviors, and she is distressed by her illness. Unfortunately, Michaela is injuring herself. Her hands are red, chapped, and raw, and her cuticles and nail beds often bleed. Her injuries are a side effect of her compulsions. When her OCD symptoms are relieved, Michaela will no longer self-harm. Treatment for Michaela will most likely involve a combination of medication and cognitive-behavioral therapy.

TRICHOTILLOMANIA: COMPULSIVE SELF-HARM

Impulse control disorders are characterized by the drive, or compulsion, to perform an act that is harmful to oneself or to others. Often, someone with an impulse control disorder feels increasingly tense before the act, and then feels a sense of relief or gratification after performing it. One specific impulse control disorder that involves physical self-harm is trichotillomania. Trichotillomania (TTM) is an impulse disorder that causes people to pull out the hair from their scalp, eyelashes, eyebrows, or other parts of the body, resulting in noticeable bald patches. Trichotillomania may appear to resemble an addiction, a tic disorder, or obsessive-compulsive disorder. To others it might just seem to be a bad habit. However, trichotillomania is a serious mental illness that causes great discomfort to many people and their families. In fact, trichotillomania is estimated to affect 1 to 2 percent of the population, or 4 to 11 million Americans.[12]

CASE STUDY: TRICHOTILLOMANIA

Katie began pulling out her hair when she was seven years old. She began by twirling and tugging a piece of it, usually from the left rear side of her head. As she continued to pull, her hairs broke, leaving her with an area of short, thin hair. Over time, she began isolating each piece of hair and pulling it out. Sometimes she would eat the hair; other times she would just inspect it, looking for split ends or wrapping it around her finger. Usually, Katie pulled her hair when she was bored or distracted; for example, while watching TV. As she got older, Katie pulled her hair when she was stressed, worried about a big test at school or her soccer tryouts. Now that Katie is 14, she is becoming more aware of her appearance and self-conscious about her hair-pulling. For the first time, she wants to stop doing it, but she is finding it increasingly difficult to resist the urges.

Katie's parents are aware of Katie's hair-pulling. However, they're becoming more concerned as they have noticed that her eyebrows are getting thinner and thinner. In fact, there are little bald patches in the arch of each eyebrow. When Katie's mom asks her about it, she denies that there is anything wrong or that she is intentionally pulling out her eyebrows. She is growing her bangs longer to cover her eyebrows but in the meantime, she uses eyebrow pencil to fill in the thin spaces. Katie is confused about why she does this and scared that she can't stop. She is thinking of talking to her best friend's mom who is a psychologist; maybe she can help her understand why she has this strange compulsion.

Trichotillomania typically begins in late childhood or early adolescence with peaks at between five and eight years and at age 13. Adult females are much more likely than adult males to experience TTM. However, among children, boys and girls are equally likely to experience the disorder. Some individuals might experience symptoms of trichotillomania for limited periods of time. For others, TTM can be a lifelong battle. Although hair-pulling is thought to be exacerbated by stress, it can also occur when one is distracted. Some people with TTM might pull their hair when they are reading or watching television.[13]

BODY DYSMORPHIC DISORDER (BDD): COMPULSIVE SELF-HARM

Someone with body dysmorphic disorder believes that there is something terribly wrong with his or her appearance and is pre-occupied by the perceived defect. This defect can be imagined, or an extreme exaggeration of a real physical attribute. Most complaints of people with BDD involve characteristics of the head or face, including thinning hair, acne, scars, wrinkles, skin discoloration, or too much facial hair. Some people with BDD are excessively concerned with the size of their nose, the shape of their eyebrows or mouth, or the color of the teeth. Many people with BDD are unhappy with more than one aspect of their appearance. They might not like their nose and the shape of their eyes.

People with BDD suffer greatly. Whereas many people are critical about some part of their appearance, most do not spend hours at home staring at themselves in the mirror every day. Someone with BDD might pick at their skin excessively, trying

Figure 3.2 Individuals with body dysmorphic disorder are overfo-
cused on a perceived physical flaw in themselves. Some may self-
harm in an attempt to fix the flaw. *Ariel Skelley/Corbis*

to clear up acne or even out their complexion. BDD can drive one to hurt oneself in an attempt to get rid of the perceived flaw or defect. As in trichotillomania, someone with BDD can become so obsessed with the shape of their eyebrows that they ultimately pluck them all. In trichotillomania, the relief comes from the process of pulling out the hair for its own sake. In BDD, the pulling of the hair is only a means to an end; to correct a flaw that is perceived as overwhelming. Individuals can become so intensely self-conscious because of BDD that they cannot leave the house for any reason as they are too ashamed about their appearance.

In extreme cases, people with BDD seek intervention from plastic surgeons or other cosmetic specialists. However, as patients they are seldom satisfied. For someone with BDD, perfection is the only acceptable outcome, but it is impossible to attain. Even if one problem is eliminated, another will undoubtedly emerge. For this reason, many people who seek plastic surgery are asked detailed questions about how their current appearance has affected their daily life. If someone has had several procedures and remains unsatisfied, psychotherapy or medication might be a safer and more effective way of dealing with the unhappiness rather than surgery or some other invasive measure.

CASE STUDY: BODY DYSMORPHIC DISORDER

Anne is a 26-year-old woman who lives in New York City. She is beautiful, successful, and has lots of friends and a loving family. To most people, Anne appears to have everything. Unfortunately, Anne is finding it more and more difficult to leave her apartment to go to work, to socialize, or to run a simple errand. Anne has never liked the way she looks. She knows that people find her attractive, but she cannot understand why. To her, her nose is too bumpy, her complexion cloudy, and her ears large and manly. She spends a lot of time and money on her appearance, but for all her effort, she always feels like a fraud. She spends hours in front of the mirror every day, pushing her nose around, squeezing her pores, and plucking her eyebrows and eyelashes. The truth is, she's making herself look and feel worse. She sometimes picks at her pores with a needle, which has ended up leaving small scars. On one occasion, Anne went too far and cut into her nose, which later became infected. She wants to stop picking at her face but she just can't stop thinking about it.

Her preoccupation with her appearance has worsened over the past few months. She is so distracted by mirrors that she avoids going to the restroom at the office for fear of being caught studying herself. She tries to forget about how bad she thinks she looks, but her self-consciousness returns quickly and with force. So far Anne hasn't had any plastic surgery, although she is saving up for a rhinoplasty. However, Anne knows that that will not solve all her problems. She'll still have other major flaws. Maybe after several surgical procedures she will feel better about herself. Having a normal life seems out of her reach now; she is too self-conscious to be around other people any more than necessary.

BORDERLINE PERSONALITY DISORDER: IMPULSIVE SELF-HARM

The only mental disorder for which self-injury is a potential diagnostic criterion is borderline personality disorder (BPD). Self-injury is not a requirement for a diagnosis of borderline personality disorder, only a marker or a possible symptom. Borderline personality disorder is marked primarily by instability of moods, self-image, and interpersonal relationships. People with BPD have an intense fear of abandonment. They can be preoccupied with worry about the end of a relationship and engage in drastic behaviors to keep loved ones close. As one might imagine, their unpredictable behavior can often have the opposite effect.

CASE STUDY: BORDERLINE PERSONALITY DISORDER

Emily is a 46-year-old elementary school teacher. She lives alone in a small apartment in Toronto. Emily is unmarried, has few friends, and doesn't speak to her parents. In general, Emily keeps to herself and lives a fairly quiet life.

Emily has a therapist with whom she has worked for 15 years. Dr. Michael Kline is Emily's one constant connection to the outside world. Michael knows a lot about Emily, some of which he suspects is not true. The picture she paints of her life is one filled with friends and excitement, although Emily has never once missed an appointment. He feels that he is the most important person in her life. What he does believe is that Emily was both sexually and physically abused as a young child, was neglected by her parents, and has a great deal of quiet rage that she inflicts upon herself. According to Emily, her mother was depressed throughout Emily's childhood. Her father was an alcoholic, and although he was financially successful, he rarely saw his children except for at dinner, which was typically accompanied by several drinks. As a result, Emily took care of her mother and avoided her father. She never felt that she was parented; instead, she felt that she was forced to be the parent for her mom and dad.

After Emily left home to go to college, she began seeing a boy who she met in an English class. After merely a few days, Emily decided she was in love with him. She talked to him about marriage, starting a family, and told him she wanted to meet his family. After about a month, the boy ended the relationship and Emily was devastated. She cried and begged him to stay with her, eventually cutting her wrists in front of him. He took her to the emergency room for the first time. This was ultimately the first of countless parasuicidal acts.

Dr. Kline has been treating Emily for borderline personality disorder. She takes an antidepressant medication and participates in groups where she learns how better to manage her pain and rage. Emily occasionally goes on dates, but the relationships always follow the same pattern. She quickly becomes obsessed and frightens the man away. Emily isn't interested in having female friends so she has no social life. Michael is the only person she talks to about personal things and she doesn't see that changing in the future.

One way in which someone with BPD may attempt to prevent a loved one from leaving is by performing self-harm. Impulsive, destructive behaviors like self-mutilation, parasuicide, binge eating and purging, drug and alcohol abuse, and promiscuity are all characteristics of borderline personality disorder. These dangerous behaviors share one dangerous potential outcome: death. As a result, BPD is one of the most lethal of all forms of mental illness. Indeed, the mental health research organization NARSAD estimates that between 3 and 9.5 percent of patients with BPD die by suicide.[14] This estimate neglects the number of people with borderline personality disorder who die as a result of drunk-driving accidents, accidental death from drugs or alcohol, or complications of sexually transmitted diseases. Suicidal gestures and self-mutilation are common in borderline personality disorder, and may be a symptom of a general problem with **impulse control**, the tendency to act spontaneously without considering the consequences.

Figure 3.3 It is not uncommon for someone who self-injures to also demonstrate disordered eating behaviors, such as characteristics of anorexia nervosa. *AP Photo/Barrett Stinson*

IMPULSIVE SELF-HARM AND EATING DISORDERS

One observation researchers have made is that self-injurers share many characteristics with people with eating disorders.[15] Eating disorders and self-harm most commonly affect young Caucasian women. One of the most severe eating disorders is bulimia nervosa. Bulimia nervosa is an eating disorder in which people eat a large amount of food in a short period of time while feeling out of control. After bingeing, someone with bulimia nervosa performs some compensatory behavior, like vomiting or exercising excessively, to make up for the calories they recently ingested. Behaviors like vomiting or taking laxatives are called purging behaviors, whereas exercising excessively or fasting are called non-purging behaviors. Some theorists believe that, like self-harm, bingeing and purging may also be associated with a problem with impulse control. Thus, bulimia nervosa and deliberate self-harm may be mediated by the same mechanism (a problem with impulse

Nail Biting: Bad Habit or Mental Illness?

Nail biting, or onychophagia, is a common behavior. Many people bite their nails when feeling stressed or anxious. Others bite their nails when they are bored or distracted by homework or watching television. Nail biting shares some characteristics with other nervous habits like thumb sucking, hair twisting, and picking at the skin.

However, some mental health professionals consider nail biting to be more serious than just a bad habit. People who chronically bite their nails have an increased risk of infection to their fingers and mouths. The spread of bacteria is facilitated by nail biting, and people who bite their nails are more likely to develop dental cavities. Many people who bite their nails cause real damage to the cuticle and soft tissue surrounding the nail. Extreme nail biting may be considered to be a form of self-mutilation. When one bites one's nails down into the nail bed, fingertips can become highly sensitive to pain. Touching acidic or salty foods like lemon juice or potato chips can become excruciatingly painful.

Presently, chronic nail biting is not recognized by the American Psychiatric Association. As a result, there are few control). Finally, there is some overlap between those who have eating disorders and those who self-harm. It is not uncommon for someone who self-injures to also demonstrate disordered eating, and vice versa.

• • • • • • • •

reliable estimates of how common the behavior is or how best to treat the problem. Young males are the largest group of nail biters, and it is estimated that between 30 and 44 percent of children and adolescents bite their fingernails. One form of treatment for extreme nail biting is called Habit Reversal Training, a four-part process that teaches one to unlearn the habit of nail biting. In some cases, medication can be helpful in treating severe nail biting. The same medications that are used to treat obsessive-compulsive disorder or trichotillomania can also help alleviate the most severe forms of nail biting. More commonly, people who want to stop biting their nails practice some form of self-administered aversion therapy. Painting one's nails with a bad-tasting nail polish or a spicy substance like Tabasco sauce can help minimize nail biting. The unpleasant taste can serve as punishment for conscious nail biting or alert the sufferer when they unconsciously put their fingers in their mouths. Finally, some people report that replacing the nail biting habit with another habit, like chewing gum, can be effective.

SUMMARY

Self-harm is associated with several psychiatric diagnoses. Developmental disorders like autism and Tourette's disorder may be marked by stereotyped self-harming behaviors such as rocking or head banging. Schizophrenia or other psychotic disorders can involve drastic and major acts of self-injury. Obsessive-compulsive disorder involves rituals that may be performed to the extent that they cause physical harm. Trichotillomania is marked by irresistible urges to pull out one's hair resulting in noticeable hair loss. Disorders in which physical appearance has an undue influence on self-esteem such as eating disorders and body dysmorphic disorder are often marked by self-harm. Finally, impulsive self-injury such as cutting or parasuicidal behaviors occurs in borderline personality disorder.

What Are the Causes of Self-Harming Behavior?

Psychologists know very little about why people practice self-harm. An **evolutionary approach** to a behavior assumes that people engage in behaviors that protect them and further their genes. Self-harm is contrary to this fundamental desire to avoid pain and experience pleasure. What would cause people to do things that damage their bodies and may result in injury or death? People who practice self-harm are part of a **heterogeneous** group. That means that there is a lot of variety among people who choose to harm themselves. For some, self-harm is a cry for help and might be a first step to a suicide attempt. For others, self-harm is a coping mechanism that makes life more bearable. Self-harm can be used as a voice; an external expression of internal pain. Some people practice self-harm for an extended period of time, perhaps over many years. Others might only experiment with self-injury, perhaps as part of a group in adolescence. Although research about the causes of self-injury is in its early stages, most scholars agree that self-harm occurs as a result of biological, psychological, and social factors.

CASE STUDY

Lynne is a 30-year-old nurse who was brought to the hospital after her most recent suicide attempt. Her family has all but given up on her, and no one comes to visit her in the hospital anymore. Her mother says that this is the eleventh time that Lynne has been taken to the hospital, this time for swallowing a bottle of Tylenol. "This wasn't for real," her mother tells the doctor. "If it was serious, she would have taken the prescription pain killers like she did last time."

Lynne has been married twice and divorced once. Her second husband left her and has not contacted her for six months. Even though she is technically married, she has a new boyfriend, Kevin, whom she met six weeks ago through an Internet dating site. Kevin left to go camping with some friends, which may have triggered this most recent suicide attempt. Lynne has no way to contact Kevin, since he doesn't have cell phone reception where he is camping. She is angry and feels isolated and believes she has no way of conveying her loneliness.

"I have always felt alone and empty," Lynne tells her therapist. "As long as I can remember. I kept trying different things to find myself, but all I find is disappointment. I think I'll be happy once I meet my soul mate. So far, I haven't had much luck, but I think Kevin could be the one. Well, he could have been, if he hadn't been so selfish to just take off with his friends with no concern for my feelings."

Lynne reports a pattern of relationship failures in which every man she has dated has disappointed her. Each relationship begins as a great romance, and then is filled with arguments that sometimes turn physical. Several times in each relationship, Lynne has either started cutting herself or has attempted suicide. She usually cuts the inside of her arms and thighs—cuts that she can keep hidden when she needs to. When Kevin left last time, Lynne carved a "K" into her abdomen and then took an overdose of painkillers. Every man she has dated has visited her in the hospital, and that's when she feels the most secure.

Because of her frequent depression and suicide attempts, it took Lynne nine years to finish nursing school. She also dropped out of school three times to try different careers. Once she joined a band as a singer and traveled around the southwestern United States playing in small bars. Another time, she decided she wanted to be a teacher and began working at a preschool. When that no longer interested her, she decided to take up painting. After she received some lukewarm feedback on some of her work, she decided that the art teacher didn't like her and dropped out of the class. After several years of floating from job to job, she became a nurse at a local hospital. Unfortunately, it has been difficult to keep a steady job at a hospital with all of the mental health days she takes. If she doesn't get out of the psychiatric hospital soon, she will most likely lose her current job.

PSYCHOLOGICAL EXPLANATIONS FOR WHY PEOPLE SELF-HARM

The Conterio and Favazza study in 1986 was one of the first studies of self-harm. The authors offered a description of the typical self-injurer. Like Lynne in the case study above, the typical self-harmer is female, in her mid-20s to early 30s, and has been hurting herself since her teens. She tends to be middle- or upper-middle-class, intelligent, well educated, and from a background of physical and/or sexual abuse or from a home with at least one alcoholic parent. These young women often reported symptoms of eating disorders.[16] Given these characteristics, many psychologists speculate about why this particular group of people may choose to engage in self-injury.

Unfortunately, the reasons for self-injurious behavior are often misunderstood. One common misconception is that self-harmers engage in these behaviors in order to receive attention. Alternatively, others might expect that someone who

Figure 4.1 A young self-harmer with visible scars. Studies indicate that people who experienced trauma in childhood may be likely to practice self-harm. *Andrew Ramsay/iStockphoto*

chooses to cut oneself must have a desire to die. According to recent research, neither of these explanations accounts for most reports of self-harm. Most people who engage in self-harm go to great lengths to cover up the evidence of their behaviors. Janis Whitlock and her colleagues at Cornell University in Ithaca, New York, revealed that 36 percent of self-injuring college students reported that they kept their self-harm a secret.[17] Their self-injury is only practiced in private, and they rarely share what they have done with friends or family. Keeping self-injurious behaviors secret may give some people a sense of control and relief from tension or sadness. In the case study in Chapter 2, Richard hurt himself when he was feeling inadequate. He found that enduring self-inflicted pain made him feel strong and in control. For Richard, self-harm was a private coping strategy, or a way of dealing with overwhelming emotions. If self-harm is viewed as a coping strategy, it cannot simultaneously be considered evidence of a wish to die. Ironically, some self-harmers report that hurting themselves makes life bearable.

CHILDHOOD ABUSE

Many studies report that people who self-harm often report childhood physical or sexual abuse.[18] In a study with those diagnosed with a personality disorder, Bessel van der Kolk and his colleagues at Boston University found 79 percent of those patients who reported cutting also reported a history of childhood abuse and 89 percent reported parental neglect.[19] Recently, Dr. Kim Gratz at the University of Maryland found that maltreatment by parents distinguished college students who self-injured from those who did not.[20] There are several reasons why people who experienced trauma in childhood might be likely to practice self-harm. Abusive families are unlikely to model or teach appropriate coping and self-soothing strategies. As a result, self-injury might be used as a way to calm oneself or cope with a difficult situation. Armando Favazza of the University of Missouri suggests that some people self-harm because it allows them to control the pain that in their childhood was uncontrollable.[21] By hurting oneself, one can gain control over experiences that were previously perceived as out of their control. Finally, for people who endured childhood abuse, self-injury might be seen as deserved punishment; pain might help ease feelings of guilt.

One way of coping with abuse or trauma is through a process called **dissociation**. Dissociation is the ability of the mind to break apart from reality, or to mentally remove oneself from a painful situation. When dissociation occurs in the extreme, the result is **dissociative identity disorder**, or what was previously called multiple personality disorder. Someone with dissociative identity disorder has split his identity or personality and has formed at least one entirely different personality. Other dissociative disorders involve **amnesia**, or significant memory loss, usually following a traumatic event.

Some people become so good at dissociating that they may report feeling "spacey" for prolonged periods of time. The practice of dissociation might begin in childhood and continue into adolescence and adulthood. Specifically, dissociation might help children deal with abusive events. In adulthood, self-injury might accompany dissociation. Alternatively, individuals may use self-injury as a means to relieve the feelings of dissociation. That is, self-harm might help bring them back to reality, or to feel alive. In 2005, Erin Polk and her colleagues at the University of Mary Washington in Virginia reported that 24 percent of self-injurers reported that they did so to stop feeling numb and to feel more alive or "real."[22]

Another explanation for self-injurious behavior comes from Todd Heatherton and Roy Baumeister of Dartmouth College. They argued that harmful behaviors like binge-eating or self-injury may be an attempt to escape from self-awareness.[23] When some people become too self-aware, or conscious of unpleasant feelings, they might choose to use harmful behaviors as a way to change their focus. In this sense, self-harm might function like drug or alcohol use. Some researchers argue that a history of childhood trauma may cause difficulty in regulating emotional experiences.[24] Specifically, Marsha Linehan of the University of Washington believes that people who self-harm have difficulty regulating their emotions. She found that most people who self-harm exhibit **mood-dependent behavior.**[25] This means that they tend to react impulsively and often inappropriately to strong feelings. For people with poor emotion regulation, self-injury might be the first coping strategy at their disposal; it might help in the short term, but it is ineffective for managing their emotions over the long term.

ALEXITHYMIA

Alexithymia is the inability to describe emotional experiences appropriately. People with alexithymia don't have the vocabulary to talk about their feelings. When one experiences something sad or upsetting, a good way to cope with negative feelings is to tell someone. Someone with alexithymia is unable to put feelings into words. An individual might be able to describe events, but the description would be bland, lacking feeling. This doesn't mean that someone with alexithymia does not feel, but that his or her feelings often remain unexpressed. Some researchers believe that there is an association between alexithymia and self-injury. One theory is that people who self-harm do so in order to release emotions. Kim Gratz of the University of Maryland reported that the inability to express feelings is related to the frequency of self-harm in college women.[26] For people with alexithymia, self-harm might help release feelings that would otherwise remain unexpressed.

BIOLOGICAL EXPLANATIONS FOR WHY PEOPLE SELF-HARM

Unfortunately, there are few studies investigating biological factors that contribute to intentional, nonsuicidal self-harm. Existing clinical studies take the approach that self-injury occurs in people who have problems with impulse control, aggressiveness, and pain perception. Because self-harm research is in its infancy, some researchers who are interested in self-harm look to people who have committed suicide to learn more about the biological origins of self-injurious behavior. There is one problem with this approach: Only a small percentage of self-injurers are suicidal. Recall that, for many, self-harm is a coping strategy. Ironically, self-injurious behaviors can make life more tolerable for some. Thus, even though self-injurious behaviors may share physical qualities with acts of suicide, the motivation behind these two kinds of behaviors can be quite different.

However, people who practice self-harm and people who commit suicide appear to share one fundamental characteristic: a problem with impulse control. Researchers have demonstrated that being impulsive, acting immediately without considering the consequences, is at least partially biologically based. Sabine Herpertz and her colleagues of the University of Aachen in Germany found that, compared to people who do not self-harm, self-harmers had both personality and biological markers of impulsivity. Self-harmers in this study reported high levels of anger, self-directed hostility, and a lack of planning.[27] Many researchers believe that self-injury emerges from a combination of poor emotion regulation and a tendency towards impulsiveness. Thus, a combination of intense, unmanageable emotions in addition to a spontaneous or impulsive personality may lead one to engage in self-harm.

THE BRAIN AND IMPULSE CONTROL

Researchers who study suicide are particularly interested in the part of the brain called the **prefrontal cortex**. The prefrontal cortex

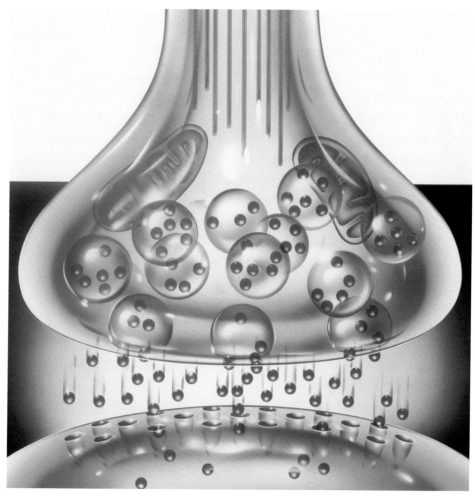

Figure 4.2 A nerve synapse. Neurotransmitters (red) are the brain's messengers, carrying information from one brain cell to the next. Low levels of serotonin, a neurotransmitter typically associated with mood, are associated with a host of psychological problems including negative mood, anxiety, and diminished impulse control. *John Bavosi/Photo Researchers, Inc.*

is the part of the brain that is found right behind your forehead. This area is responsible for coordinating thought and behavior. When you consider doing something, it is your prefrontal cortex that helps you decide whether it is a good or bad idea. Assume

(continues on page 62)

Phineas Gage

The story of Phineas Gage offers a gruesome yet compelling portrait of the intricate relationship between brain and behavior. On September 13th, 1848, Gage, a railroad foreman, was working on the tracks in Cavendish, Vermont. On this day, his duties involved filling a hole with gunpowder, adding a fuse, and then packing in sand with a tamping iron. His life was changed forever when he forgot to add the sand to one hole and used the rod to pack the gunpowder directly. The rod sparked against the rock, causing the gunpowder to ignite and blowing the rod through the front of his head. The iron rod, about three feet long and an inch and a half in diameter, entered his face beneath the left cheekbone and exited through his anterior frontal cortex, or the top front of his head. After a few minutes Gage regained consciousness, began speaking, and returned home to his boarding house, where his wounds were bandaged and he was cared for by a doctor.

A few months later Phineas Gage returned to work after what appeared to be a complete recovery, except for loss of vision in the left eye. Over time, however, people noticed that Gage seemed to undergo a personality change. According to his doctor, Mr. Gage was a hard worker and liked by his peers prior to his accident. After the accident, he became irrational, argumentative, prone to using bad language, impatient, and often stubborn. Ultimately, he became a circus sideshow act for P.T. Barnum, carrying the iron that penetrated his skull. After a few years working as a driver and on a farm, Phineas Gage died at 37 after having a series of seizures, which were suspected to have been related to his injury.

The case of Phineas Gage offered insight into the compartmentalization of the brain. Presently, neuroscientists have a

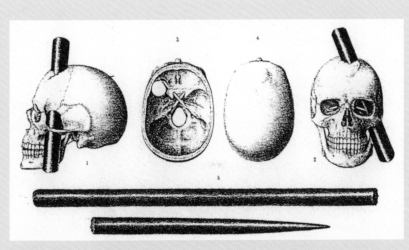

Figure 4.3 An 1850 artist's interpretation of the skull of Phineas Gage, who made headlines in 1848 when he survived an accident that left a hole in his head. Though the holes in his head eventually healed, the brain injury changed his personality. Scientists now know that damage to the frontal lobes can alter personality and impulse control without impairing basic bodily processes like breathing and digestion. *Associated Press*

basic understanding of what part of the brain is implicated in certain functions or behaviors. However, in 1850, people knew little about just how the brain worked. An injury like the one suffered by Phineas Gage would have been thought to kill him. We now understand that damage to the frontal lobes can alter personality and impulse control without impairing basic bodily processes like breathing, heart rate, or digestion. Antonio Damasio, now at the University of Southern California, has written extensively on Gage and has focused on the role of the frontal lobes on the coordination of emotion, thinking, and behavior. The frontal lobes, Damasio argues, are crucial for decision-making. According to Damasio, the story of Phineas Gage plays a crucial role historically for the understanding of the biological bases of social behavior.

(continued from page 59)

that a friend of yours takes a drink of your soda without asking. You may become annoyed and want to yell at her. Instead, you take the drink back and place it out of her reach. If your prefrontal cortex was injured or impaired in some way, you might feel compelled to scream at your friend, or worse yet, to grab your soda or hit her. Fortunately you have impulse control, due in large part to your prefrontal cortex, and are able to weigh the pros and cons of such an act of aggression.

Neurotransmitters are effectively the "messengers" of the brain, carrying information from one brain cell to another. Brain cells, called **neurons**, are sensitive to different kinds of neurotransmitters and have receptors built specifically for them. When there is an imbalance of a neurotransmitter—that is, too little or too much—behavior is affected. **Serotonin** is a neurotransmitter that is typically associated with mood. Low serotonin activity is associated with a host of psychological problems including negative mood, anxiety, and diminished impulse control. Analysis of the brains of suicide victims reveals that there are fewer neurons that release serotonin in the prefrontal cortex.

Another way of studying neurotransmitters is through measuring their **metabolites**, the substance that remains in the body after a neurotransmitter is used. The metabolite of serotonin, **5-HIAA**, can be found and measured in our **cerebrospinal fluid**, the fluid we have in our spinal column and in the ventricles of our brain. People who have committed suicide have lower levels of 5-HIAA in their cerebral spinal fluid, indicating that their brains are using less serotonin than people who die by means other than suicide.

THE BRAIN AND PAIN

Childhood trauma, especially physical and sexual abuse or neglect, can be associated with self-harm. Interestingly, animal studies have linked early psychological trauma with repetitive self-injurious behavior. Early social isolation of nonhuman primates has been related to self-injury. Specifically, rhesus monkeys kept apart from mothers and other monkeys engage in several forms of self-injurious behavior, including head banging, self-biting, self-slapping, and eye gouging.[28]

Some investigators speculate that the link between social/maternal contact in childhood and self-injury lies in the developing opioid system. **Endogenous opioids** are chemicals, like endorphins, that are produced in the body and that help relieve pain. **Opiates**, like heroin or morphine, are artificial opioids, and help relieve pain in much the same way as endogenous opioids. Breast milk contains substances that are digested and turned into opioids. **Nonnutritive sucking**, like sucking one's thumb or a pacifier, may trigger a similarly pain-relieving response. The opioid system is thought to be immature at birth and to develop according to nutrition and maternal stimulation. Children who do not receive enough social reinforcement from caregivers might become "opioid addicted" and perform self-stimulatory behaviors in order to obtain that analgesic effect. According to this theory, people who self-harm might do so in order to generate an opioid response, or a rush of analgesia after inflicting bodily pain.

People differ in their tolerance for pain. For example, some people dread having their blood drawn. The pinch of the needle can be very painful. Other people, like professional athletes, can continue strenuous physical activity even with an injured muscle or a broken bone. Dr. Robert Dworkin at the University of Rochester has reported that people with schizophrenia may be less sensitive to pain than people without these conditions.[29] Further, this pain insensitivity may be partially hereditary. Jill Hooley and her colleagues at Harvard University found that relatives of people with schizophrenia had a higher pain threshold

Figure 4.4 Animal studies have linked early psychological trauma with self-harm. Young rhesus monkeys kept apart from their mothers and other monkeys engage in various forms of self-injurious behavior, including head banging, self-biting, self-slapping, and eye gouging. *Neal McClimon/iStockphoto*

and higher pain tolerance than people without schizophrenia in their families.[30] Although this might help explain self-harm in people with psychotic disorders, it does not help us understand why otherwise healthy people choose to practice self-injury. More research needs to be done to determine if people who practice intentional self-injury respond to pain differently than people who do not self-harm.

SOCIAL INFLUENCES ON SELF-HARM

Most behaviors emerge from a combination of biological, psychological, and social influences. You have read about how psychological phenomena like dissociation might cause one to self-harm. Next, you learned about how brain processes, like the function of the serotonin neurotransmitter, are related to impulse control that might be linked to self-injury. Social influences, like one's peer group or the media, provide the final piece of the puzzle in discovering the origins of self-harm.

Adolescents are especially interested in what their peers think of them, and many shape their behavior according to what they think will help make them popular. Teenagers share information incessantly. The Internet and mobile phones have made instant communication a way of life. Virtual bulletin boards, or Internet chat rooms, can help adolescents who feel troubled or isolated connect with other teens who are suffering. While connection with others can be positive, negative consequences can emerge when teenagers share destructive coping mechanisms. Some researchers worry that the practice of self-harm is spreading rapidly among adolescents due in part to this social contagion effect. When troubled teens communicate, they might tell each other how self-harm helps them, how to practice it, and how best to cover it up.

The spread of self-harm has been likened to the proliferation of eating disorders in the 1980s and 1990s. In the early 1990s, Joan Jacobs Brumberg of Cornell University in Ithaca, New York, suggested that eating disorders were on the rise due to heightened cultural visibility of the syndromes.[31] Celebrities who are unnaturally thin appeared on the covers of major magazines and became the subject of made-for-TV movies. Actresses like Calista Flockhart and Lara Flynn Boyle achieved great success in the 1990s and were simultaneously the focus of media attention for their extremely thin bodies. Ironically, even treatment for eating disorders contributed to the spread of symptoms. Clinicians observed that patients being treated for eating disorders were being made worse by group therapy

(continues on page 68)

Peer Pressure: Why Some Teenagers Choose to Hurt Themselves

Many parents worry about their children spending time with the wrong crowd or meeting other children who have a bad influence on others. What many parents do not understand is that adolescent brain development ensures that peers take on a profound importance in middle and high school. Most kids emerge from adolescence unscathed. Others choose to engage in risky behaviors just because their friends are doing them.

Dr. Abigail Baird at Vassar College in Poughkeepsie, New York, studies the adolescent brain and is interested in why teenagers make bad decisions. One of her studies utilizes a paradigm called the "good decision, bad decision" task. Adolescent participants are asked to decide if several behaviors are good or bad ideas. Examples of such behaviors include swimming with sharks, eating a salad, setting one's hair on fire, or getting exercise. On the surface, the answers to these behaviors seem very obvious. In general, it is a bad idea to set your hair on fire and a good idea to eat a salad. However, Dr. Baird and her colleagues found that compared to adults, teenagers took a lot longer to decide what was a bad idea. Dr. Baird interpreted these results to mean that teenagers think a lot before making a big decision, although they usually end up making the right one.

However, Dr. Baird's research also speaks to the power of one's peer group in decision-making. She believes that social information is as important as oxygen to middle and high school kids. The presence of peers in the room while one is making a decision can affect the process and outcome of decision-making. In another study, Dr. Baird invited adolescents to come to the lab and answer questions on a Web site about their favorite things and activities. Examples of such questions included, "What is your favorite type of music?" The first time the adolescents answered these questions, they believed their answers were merely recorded on the Web site and that they were anonymous. When they answered the questions the first time, a brain scan revealed that a certain part of their brain was active. The second time the adolescents answered these questions, they were told that they were online with many other community teenagers. When the participants answered the questions the second time, and believed that their peers saw their responses, a different part of the brain was activated. This indicates the influence of the social situation on the brain's response.

The power of one's peer group in adolescence is huge. Peer pressure is usually a good thing. Teenagers learn how to participate in social relationships and they learn valuable lessons like how to negotiate conflict and how to solve problems. They have support when there are problems at home and ultimately learn how to have a successful romantic relationship, the foundation of a family. Unfortunately, peer pressure can sometimes lead kids to make bad choices. If a friend is practicing an unhealthy behavior, it somehow becomes more acceptable. Having a good understanding of what is appropriate for oneself, and an appreciation for the fact that there are always other kids who share one's opinions, can help teenagers get out of unhealthy peer relationships and prevent unsafe behaviors.

(continued from page 65)

sessions. In treatment, patients share information about how they binged, purged, or maintained their low weight. Patients could effectively learn new ways of maintaining and hiding their symptoms from others in their treatment setting. In the last few years, pro-eating disorder Web sites have emerged on the Internet. These Web sites provide a forum for people with eating disorders to share their behaviors with others. Called pro-Ana (for anorexia) and pro-Mia (for bulimia), these dangerous Web sites communicate harmful and potentially deadly information about how to maintain eating disorder symptoms. Sufferers encourage each other in their self-starvation and share ways to keep their behaviors secret.

More recently, Web sites about self-harm have emerged on the Internet and researchers are concerned about the extent to which they encourage self-injury. Dr. Janis Whitlock and her colleagues at Cornell University investigated how adolescents share information about self-harm on the Internet. Whitlock and her colleagues identified more than 400 Web sites dedicated to self-harm and found that most Web site users were female and between the ages of 12 and 20. The researchers concluded that while the Web sites provided troubled teens access to others who were experiencing similar difficulties, they also provided teens with new harmful behaviors to increase their self-injury repertoire.[32]

• • • • • • • •

SUMMARY

People who self-harm are a heterogenous group; no two people are identical. Although the majority of self-harmers appear to be young females, self-injury can occur in both genders, in all cultures, and at any age. Many self-harmers appear to have suffered physical and/or sexual abuse in childhood. Biological characteristics like decreased serotonin or an abnormal pain response have been associated with self-harm. Finally, the Internet, while a potentially positive vehicle for sharing information about self-injury, might actually increase the prevalence and frequency of these harmful behaviors.

5 Identification and Treatment of Self-Harm

People who self-harm can go to great lengths to hide their injurious behaviors. Self-harm can become a coping strategy, an act of self-punishment, or an addiction. Many are embarrassed or even ashamed of their behaviors and do not want to admit that they lack control over their own behavior. As a result, many self-harmers do not seek treatment. When someone does seek help for self-harm, they usually have a primary complaint of a mood or anxiety disorder. Additionally, self-harm might be a sign of a developmental or psychotic disorder. Currently, clinicians employ a host of treatment strategies, including medication and psychotherapy, to help deal with self-harm and the psychological complaints that accompany such behaviors.

> **CASE STUDY**
>
> Rebecca is a 33-year-old woman who lives with her parents. Although she is bright and attended college, she works only two days a week as a choir director for an elementary school. Rebecca is significantly overweight and has battled with her weight since adolescence. She has tried multiple diets and has successfully lost weight many times, but always seems to gain it back again. When she diets, she finds herself obsessing about food, and this obsession always leads to a binge-eating episode. In a typical binge, Rebecca will go to a drive through at a fast-food restaurant and get a large hamburger and an

extra-large french fries that she follows with a half-gallon of chocolate-chip ice cream. She will eat all this food in about 20 minutes, after which she feels terrible about herself and vows never to binge again. Unfortunately, following each binge she tries to fast by not consuming anything except green tea. Each fast inevitably leads to another binge episode. Rebecca has maintained this binge-fast routine for about 15 years.

Over the last 10 years Rebecca has also developed a drinking problem. Because she only drinks at night, she isn't concerned that she is an alcoholic. She drinks with her mother, and every two days they finish a large bottle of vodka between them. Rebecca's father is concerned about their drinking but doesn't want to sound preachy. After all, he smokes cigarettes, so it's not like he is without his vices.

Although her parents know about Rebecca's binge eating and drinking, they don't know that she hurts herself. She has worked hard to keep her self-harm a secret because she knows her parents won't understand. She has scars from her cutting and burning up and down her arms and legs. No one ever sees them because her clothing covers them. She started hurting herself when she was eight years old, right after her grandparents visited from Arkansas. During their visit, Rebecca's grandfather slipped into her room at night and sexually abused her. Although he didn't threaten her, Rebecca never told anyone about the abuse. And now, 25 years later, she is ashamed that she didn't stop it.

At 33, Rebecca is feeling more depressed than ever before. She has no friends and spends all her time with her mother or talking in chat rooms on the Internet. She has started an online romance with a man in another state who is now talking about coming to visit her. The possibility that she will have to meet him, face to face, makes her incredibly anxious. Still, she doesn't want to stop their communication entirely because it is the only connection she has to the outside world. He is getting more and more persistent about their meeting, and Rebecca just doesn't know what to do. She is ashamed of her appearance, of her body, and of the fact that she lives with her parents. Her life feels entirely out of control. Rebecca is in a great deal of pain—she feels isolated, depressed, and afraid. So far, the only way she has coped is by numbing herself to pain with food, alcohol, and self-harm. She needs to talk so someone, get some sort of help, but she doesn't know where to start.

ASSESSMENT: IDENTIFYING PEOPLE WHO SELF-HARM

The first step in securing treatment for people who practice self-harm is to determine the cause and maintenance of the behavior. Many people who practice self-harm are embarrassed or reluctant to talk about their self-harm. Some might not consider their self-injury to be a problem. Assessment of self-harm or identification of the behaviors begins with a general inquiry about the presence of self-harm. Daphne Simeon and Eric Hollander of Mount Sinai School of Medicine in New York City encourage mental health workers to ask all incoming patients, "Have you ever intentionally hurt yourself in any way?" This question can start a dialogue about self-harm and a clinician can determine whether or not self-injury should be a focus of treatment. If a patient acknowledges that they have practiced self-harm, it can be helpful to use an interview including questions about the motivation behind, frequency, and severity of self-harm. Here are examples of interview questions that can be used to assess self-harm. [33]

1. Have you ever intentionally hurt yourself in any way?
2. When you hurt yourself, did you intend to commit suicide?

3. How old were you when you first intentionally hurt yourself?
4. On average, how frequently do you hurt yourself?
5. Has your self-harm resulted in any medical interventions or complications?
6. How do you feel before you hurt yourself?
7. How do you feel after you hurt yourself?
8. Do you ever have an urge to hurt yourself?
9. Do you want to stop hurting yourself?
10. Have you ever successfully refrained from hurting yourself?
11. Do you ever use drugs or alcohol before you hurt yourself?
12. Do you know of anyone in your family who has also intentionally hurt themselves?
13. Have you ever been treated for self-injury? If so, how?

Once a pattern of self-harm has been established, a clinician can decide upon the most effective treatment plan. Before treatment can begin, a mental health worker will try to determine what category best describes the patient's self-injury: stereotypic, major, compulsive, or impulsive. Chapter 3 briefly described treatment options for stereotypic, major, and compulsive self-injury. The following section will cover treatment options for impulsive self-harm.

TREATMENT

Impulsive self-injury is a heterogeneous phenomenon. This means that people who practice impulsive self-harm do so for a variety of reasons and their experiences with self-harm reflect their differences. Typically, a self-harmer experiences an upsetting event (perhaps being rejected by a friend or romantic partner), feels increasingly **dysphoric**, tries to resist hurting herself, cannot resist, and subsequently self-injures, after which she feels relief. Medication can help alleviate the anxiety or depression that typically accompanies impulsive self harm. However, the complicated emotions surrounding impulsive self-harm make psychotherapy an essential component of successful treatment. Because self-injury is often viewed as a coping mechanism for people who lack the ability to express their emotions, it is critical that self-harmers learn alternative, less-destructive methods of communicating how they feel.

MEDICATION

There is no medication that is specifically designed to treat self-injury. In fact, there is very little research investigating the efficacy of medication in the treatment of self-harm. Instead, medications that have been demonstrated to be effective in treating negative mood states like anxiety or depression are often used to help people who practice self-harm. Medications that help alleviate self-harm work by affecting the activity of neurotransmitters. Neurotransmitters are effectively the "messengers" of the brain, carrying information from one brain cell to another. Brain cells, called neurons, are sensitive to different kinds of neurotransmitters and have receptors built specifically for them. Neurons that are sensitive to specific neurotransmitters tend to cluster together, creating circuits in the brain that help spread information.

Neurotransmitters begin their journey in **vesicles** (sacs) at the ends of neurons called the **presynaptic terminal**. An electric current is released down the **axon** and signals for the release of neurotransmitter. The vesicles are incorporated into the cell membrane, and the neurotransmitters are released into the space between two neurons, called the **synapse**. In the synapse, the neurotransmitters attach, or bind, to the receptors at the ends of another neuron, thus affecting this new neuron. The

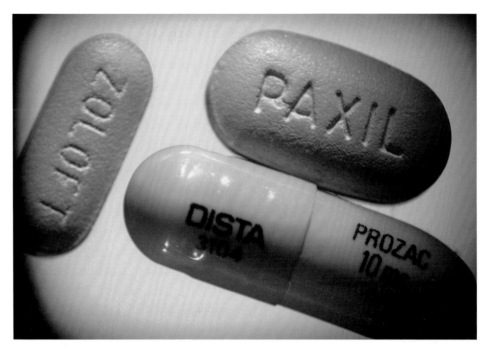

Figure 5.1 Selective serotonin reuptake inhibitors (SSRIs) such as Proazc, Paxil, and Zoloft have been found to improve mood, thereby reducing anxiety and depression. SSRIs are often used to help people who practice self-harm. *Leonard Lessin, FBPA/Photo Researchers, Inc.*

new neuron takes in as much of the neurotransmitter as it can and then releases the excess. The excess is released back into the synaptic cleft and is reabsorbed by the first neuron, a process known as **reuptake**.

There are many different neurotransmitters in the brain. One that has been implicated in self-harm is serotonin. Serotonin affects mood, behaviors, and thoughts. Low serotonin activity is associated with impulsive behaviors and unstable moods. Alternatively, high levels of serotonin have been associated with anxious or compulsive behaviors. Serotonin has been implicated in depression and may play a role in many personality disorders.

All medications for psychiatric conditions work by increasing or decreasing the availability or flow of certain neurotransmitters. Some drugs block production of a specific neurotransmitter. Others block neuron receptors, thus stopping the effect of the neurotransmitter. These drugs are called neurotransmitter **antagonists**. Another form of medication works by blocking reuptake. Blocking reuptake prevents the first neuron from taking back the extra neurotransmitter that was released into the synaptic cleft. This is how the most popular medications for depression work. Perhaps you have heard of the class of medications called **selective-serotonin reuptake inhibitors (SSRIs)**. The SSRIs have received a lot of attention in the media and have brand names like Prozac, Paxil, and Zoloft. These medications work by increasing the amount of neurotransmitter in the synapse that sends a signal to the receiving neuron. By increasing the amount of neurotransmitter, the neuron can then fire more frequently and increase the activity in brain circuits that are related to a sense of well-being. Some medications, such as the SSRIs, have been found to improve mood, thereby reducing anxiety and depression. An added benefit of these medications is that they can prevent harmful impulsive behaviors such as impulsive overeating, self-injury, and uncontrollable rage.

CASE STUDY

Marilyn is a 48-year-old mother of three. Her children are all out of the house now, and she is experiencing the "empty nest" syndrome. Her husband died of prostate cancer 10 years ago, and although Marilyn has dated a few men, for the most part, she is on her own. Although Marilyn always struggled with depression and anxiety, lately her behaviors have become even more erratic and her children are concerned about her.

For the past year, Marilyn has spent increasing amounts of time online. She buys and sells items on eBay, posts messages regularly on several Internet forums, and occasionally gambles. Marilyn has a vast network of virtual friends, whom she feels understand her and don't judge her.

Marilyn e-mails all three of her children regularly. However, when one does not respond immediately, Marilyn becomes frantic and often angry. An attractive woman, Marilyn has never had a problem getting the attention she desires. When she does not receive this attention, especially from her children, she feels rejected and alone. She has been struggling with urges to hurt herself, which she is frequently unable to resist. If she becomes upset and doesn't self-injure, she sends some very cruel messages to her daughter, in which she calls her daughter ugly names and claims to have never loved her. Marilyn is less aggressive toward her older son, instead using manipulative suicidal threats to get him to come home and visit her. Marilyn virtually ignores her youngest son, whom she feels reminds her of her husband.

Marilyn's latest outburst has all three of her children worried and confused. After not hearing from any of her children in 24 hours, she decided to carve the initials of her oldest son and daughter into her forearm. After she did so, she took photographs and emailed them to her children. She told them that she wanted them to see on the outside the pain that she felt on the inside. Naturally, her children were horrified and immediately met to discuss the most appropriate next step. They agreed that Marilyn needed immediate psychiatric help, but they were uncertain how best to get her to agree to treatment.

Marilyn exhibits several signs of the typical impulsive self-harmer. When she experiences an upsetting event, like her children not responding to her e-mails, she feels compelled to cut herself. An interpersonal rejection is immediately followed by an aggressive act, either toward her children or herself. Her pain has escalated to the point at which she feels she needs to hurt herself in order to express to others how she feels. Marilyn desperately needs psychiatric help before her self-harm does irreparable harm. Unfortunately, there is no psychotherapeutic technique uniquely designed for people who practice self-harm. Instead, many self-harmers are treated with an approach usually used for people with borderline personality disorder. An appropriate treatment program for Marilyn will likely include psychotherapy as well as medication.

PSYCHODYNAMIC PSYCHOTHERAPY

Many consider Sigmund Freud the father of modern psychology. An Austrian neurologist and psychiatrist, Freud created **psychoanalysis**, a therapeutic technique based upon the assumption that all mental pathology originates in childhood and is driven by the unconscious. The unconscious, according to Freud, houses the drives, desires and needs of human life. From far beneath the surface, the unconscious directs behavior, and sometimes clinical symptoms appear.

Psychoanalysis is still used today by a select few of mental health practitioners. Other therapists acknowledge Freud's influence but do not strictly follow his theories. Instead, a technique known as *psychodynamic psychotherapy* is used to help many people uncover reasons why they engage in harmful and maladaptive behaviors.

The goal of a psychodynamic approach to self-harm is to identify and challenge the unconscious thoughts and feelings that contribute to self-harm. Effectively, this is making the unconscious conscious. Because so many self-harmers hurt themselves due to a lack of appropriate coping methods for dealing with overwhelming emotions, it can be very helpful for a therapist to help develop a language for the feelings that underlie self-harm. A psychodynamic approach to self-harm views self-injurious behaviors as violent and hostile attack behaviors. Part of the challenge of therapy involves identification of the object of the anger (for example, the self, the body, the mother, the friend, or the romantic partner) and discovery of a more appropriate way to cope with it. The environment surrounding acts of self-harm can be very important. A skilled therapist will want to know about interpersonal events that occurred before the act and what kind of feelings accompanied them. Finally, an important part of all types of treatment for people who practice self-harm involves learning to anticipate when one feels like they want to hurt themselves and considering alternative activities. Some therapists suggest behaviors that have a physical component, like holding an ice cube or taking a hot shower. These actions can make one feel strong physical sensations without being harmful. By engaging in these types of behaviors, one might successfully and safely derail self-harming impulses.

TREATMENT FOR BORDERLINE PERSONALITY DISORDER AND SELF-HARM

Self-harm, specifically self-mutilation, has been linked to borderline personality disorder. John Gunderson and Perry Hoffman at McLean Hospital in Belmont, Massachusetts, emphasize the connection between BPD and self-mutilation and cite studies that report that approximately 80 percent of BPD patients have practiced self-mutilation at some point in their lives.[34] Many theorists consider self-harm to be an indicator of possible borderline pathology. Although all people who self-harm do not necessarily have borderline personality disorder, many self-harmers receive treatment alongside people with BPD. Dr. Otto Kernberg, professor of psychiatry at Cornell

University and director of the Institute for Personality Disorders at Cornell-Weill Medical Center, has developed a treatment program for people with borderline personality disorder that also addresses self-harming behaviors. Kernberg's approach to treating BPD, and self-harm, is by using transference-focused therapy. **Transference** is a psychoanalytic term meaning the unconscious redirection of feelings for one person to another. An example of this is when a wife unconsciously feels like she is being parented by her husband and as a result, rages against him like she is a child. Although she is an adult, she is transferring the anger she feels for her father to her husband. In psychoanalytic or psychodynamic psychotherapy, the therapist becomes the transferred-to agent. Essentially, a man who feels rejected by a friend or family member might later take innocuous behaviors by his therapist to mean that she is rejecting him. Transference, in a therapeutic setting, can be a safe and healthy way to work out upsetting interpersonal problems.

One characteristic of borderline personality disorder is having problems in personal relationships. It is difficult for someone with BPD to maintain a relationship, and their inability to manage their emotions appropriately often leads to self-harm. Kernberg takes a zero-tolerance approach to self-injury. That means that once a patient has engaged in self-harm, she cannot call the therapist for assistance for a specific period of time. Therapeutic intervention must come before the self-injurious act, not immediately following. Therapy, particularly for someone with BPD, can be especially meaningful to the patient. By setting limits about how self-harm is treated in a therapeutic context, the clinician can effectively punish self-injurious behavior.

DIALECTICAL BEHAVIOR THERAPY

The most empirically well-established treatment for borderline personality disorder is called **dialectical behavior therapy (DBT)**.

Figure 5.2 In dialectical behavior therapy (DBT), group therapy involves learning to manage out-of-control emotions and difficult relationships. DBT is the only treatment that has been found to effectively reduce the incidence and frequency of self-mutilation associated with borderline personality disorder. *Richard T. Nowitz/Photo Researchers, Inc.*

Marsha Linehan of the University of Washington in Seattle is the creator of DBT and one of the leaders in BPD research. DBT was originally designed to treat people who engaged in parasuicidal behaviors, or self-injury with questionable suicidal intent. Over time, it became apparent that most people who practiced parasuicide also suffered from borderline personality disorder, and the treatment was adjusted accordingly. Dialectical behavior therapy is based on the premise that people with borderline personality disorder have two major problems: emotional dysregulation and limited problem-solving skills. According to

(continues on page 85)

Body Modification

Tattoos and body-piercing are a common phenomenon. One study in 2003 indicated that 16 percent of American adults have at least one tattoo. Body-piercing, particularly piercing of the ears, has been practiced universally for thousands of years. More extreme forms of body modification, such as full body tattoos or large-scale or genital piercing, are rare. Some people engage in body modification for aesthetic or artistic expression, effectively using their body as a canvas. Others drastically modify their bodies to show identification with a particular group, religious or otherwise. Addiction to body modification, perhaps to the rush of endorphins that accompany pain, can drive people to engage in body modification to the extreme. Some forms of body modification are disturbing to people, whereas others are so commonplace that they rarely are noticed.

Figure 5.3 Some forms of body modification are relatively common and culturally accepted. *Stephen Stickler/Corbis*

One form of body modification that is the subject of controversy is male circumcision. Male circumcision is the removal of the foreskin of the penis. Historically, members of many religious and cultural groups were mandated to perform this procedure at different points in life. Today, it is common for infant males to be circumcised, whereas in some tribal cultures, circumcision is a rite of passage in adolescence. Some groups strongly object to male circumcision, calling it barbaric and cruel. Others cite medical and hygienic reasons for maintaining the practice, and claim that infants have no

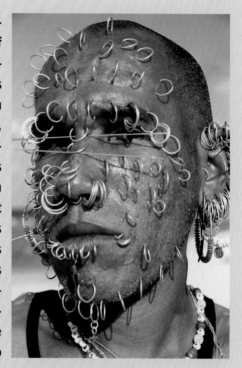

Figure 5.4 Extreme body modification. Some researchers who are interested in self-harm are also interested in what makes one take drastic, often painful measures to physically alter one's appearance. *Joel W. Rogers/Corbis*

memory of the procedure. A *New York Times* article from March 29, 2007, cited a study that found that circumcised men were 50 percent less likely to be infected with HIV from heterosexual partners, and revealed that the World Health Organization was officially encouraging circumcision for men to reduce risk of HIV infection.

Another form of body modification that many find disturbing is called tongue bifurcation or tongue splitting. Tongue splitting is the process of cutting the tongue from the tip back toward the

(continued)

base. The ultimate result is a forked tongue, much like a snake. Tongue splitting should be performed only by a physician, and few physicians are willing to perform this procedure.

There are a few extreme body-modifiers who are celebrated in the body modification community. Erik Sprague, a 35-year-old sideshow performer, is better known by his stage name, the Lizard Man. Until he began practicing extreme body modification, Sprague was a graduate student at the University of Albany. Among his most immediately apparent features, the Lizard Man has sharpened teeth, a forked tongue, and all-over body tattoos. His tattoos include scales to give his skin the appearance of a lizard. He had small ridges implanted into his eyebrows to give them a bumpy appearance. His earlobes, nipples, and nose are pierced. The Lizard Man performs all over the world and is considered by many in the community to be an example of excellence in body modification.

Body modification takes many forms. A majority of girls and women now pierce their ears, and piercing is not unusual in young men. People seldom take notice of tattoos except when they are covering one's face. However, at what point does body modification become extreme? Can one become addicted to drastically altering their appearance? Are there personality characteristics that define people who are more open to body modification practices? Finally, are people who self-harm more likely to engage in body modification procedures? These are all questions that remain unanswered. Some researchers who are interested in self-harm are also interested in what makes one take drastic, often painful measures to physically alter their appearance.

(continued from page 81)

the theoretical foundation upon which DBT is built, problems with aggression, rage, and self-harm are symptoms of greater problems with controlling, managing, and expressing one's emotions. People with BPD who self-harm can do so in order to help manage their own emotional pain as well as to influence others to attend to their needs.

Thus far, DBT is the only treatment that has been found to be effective at reducing the incidence and frequency of all forms of self-mutilation associated with BPD.[35] Dialectical behavioral therapy is a one-year outpatient program. This means that DBT patients live at home and go to a treatment center for all DBT meetings. Patients enrolled in DBT take part in two activities. The first involves weekly individual psychotherapy. The individual therapy sessions provide immediate support by way of the therapeutic relationship and a context in which one can practice new interpersonal and coping skills. Outside of therapy, DBT therapists are available to the patient by phone. A patient is encouraged to call their therapist if they feel the urge to self-harm. The second part of DBT involves group therapy sessions. Group therapy sessions involve social-skills training, a practical problem-solving approach to managing out-of-control emotions and difficult relationships. Reducing the frequency of self-harm requires learning better ways to cope with negative feelings. Both components of DBT help patients learn about why they self-harm and employ alternative strategies.

Treating someone with self-harm is a complicated process. Because self-harm research is still in its infancy, most practitioners rely on established methods of treating borderline personality disorder to address problems with self-injury. Like people with BPD, many of those who self-harm have poor impulse control, overwhelming emotions, and limited techniques for coping with strong feelings. Psychotherapy for people with BPD addresses many issues that are shared by people who self-harm.

• • • • • • • •

SUMMARY

The first step in providing treatment for people who practice self-harm is identification of the problem. Mental health clinicians are encouraged to ask all people entering treatment if they have ever physically harmed themselves intentionally. Although there is no one medication known to effectively "cure" self-harm, several antidepressant medications, like the selective-serotonin reuptake inhibitors, have been shown to be somewhat effective at preventing these behaviors. People who practice self-harm typically do so for complicated reasons. Thus, psychotherapy is often used in addition to medication to help people learn better ways of coping with and expressing strong feelings. Two established treatment programs for people with borderline personality disorder, dialectical behavior therapy and transference-focused psychotherapy, address self-injury directly and can be used with people who practice impulsive self-harm regularly.

Prevention: How Do We Prevent Self-Harm?

People who practice self-harm do so for a variety of reasons. A biological predisposition toward impulsiveness, exposure to trauma in childhood, and difficulty coping with strong emotions may all contribute to one's tendency to engage in self-harm. Some people, primarily teenagers, experiment with self-harm because they see other kids doing it. With such a heterogeneous group, how can our society work to prevent these dangerous and sometimes lethal behaviors?

CASE STUDY

Taylor is 14 years old and just starting the 10th grade. Although she is not the most popular girl in school, she is well-liked and has several good friends. The move from middle school to the high school is a big one, and Taylor, like the other girls, wants this year to be different. Taylor has decided that she wants to be part of the more popular group, and she is going to figure out a way to fit in.

Over the summer, Taylor grew up a lot. She was away at a tennis camp for eight weeks and became very fit and tanned. Her long hair became highlighted naturally, and all in all, Taylor became very beautiful very quickly. The "queen bees" at her school took notice of her immediately and asked her to join their group. Taylor happily agreed.

Taylor is on the honor roll and the tennis team. She has worked hard in school and her parents are very proud of her. However, by the time Christmas vacation arrived, they noticed that Taylor was looking different from how she did just six months earlier. She was wearing lower-rise jeans, tighter T-shirts, and a lot more makeup. She was spending more and more time with one new girlfriend, Cherrie, and her parents were becoming worried about her.

Cherrie lives alone with her aunt. Her father left her mother when Cherrie was just six weeks old and her mother died a year later. Although reluctant to do so, Cherrie's Aunt Susan obtained custody of her when she was an infant. Susan got married when Cherrie was eight, but was divorced a year later. There has been very little consistency in Cherrie's life, and she has grown up very fast. She began dieting by the time she was 10 and drinking alcohol by age 12. At 13, she started cutting herself on occasion and pierced her own ears. Cherrie is a pretty girl, although she looks about five years older than she is. Popular in her high school, Cherrie is the topic of a lot of gossip, and simultaneously the subject of envy of many other girls.

Cherrie and Taylor's friendship has flourished fast. Taylor has seen Cherrie's home life and feels sorry for her. Cherrie envies Taylor's stable upbringing and often asks to sleep over at Taylor's house. One day Taylor was shocked to see Cherrie cutting herself with a safety pin. Cherrie told her how good it makes her feel and suggested that Taylor try it. Although initially hesitant, Taylor cut the inside of her arm once and was surprised that the pain wasn't as bad as she expected it to be.

Taylor is one of thousands of adolescents who have experimented with self-harm. Whether self-harm becomes a chronic problem for Taylor depends upon many factors. Her relationship with her family, her peers, and her own sense of self can help

Taylor figure out why there are better ways to cope with problems than by injuring herself.

PUBLIC HEALTH

Mental health practitioners such as psychologists, psychiatrists, and social workers are interested in identifying people who practice self-harm and treating them successfully. Essentially, clinicians try to help people learn to deal with bad feelings appropriately. Researchers who study self-harm are interested in figuring out why someone would choose to self-injure as well as determining what features contribute to an effective treatment program. Another way to examine a problem like self-harm is through a **public health** approach. Someone who studies self-harm from a public health approach views self-harm as a threat to the community as a whole. As such, a public health worker wants to figure out how to prevent self-harm in the community and effectively eradicate the problem.

Public health programs have made tremendous progress in eliminating disease and promoting health worldwide. The use of appropriate sanitation measures, the administration of vaccines, and making seatbelts in cars mandatory are all ways in which public health programs have helped save millions of lives. Additionally, there are public health programs directed toward mental health issues. One example of such a program is ensuring that people of all income levels receive access to quality psychiatric care. Another way a public health program can be used is to bring a new problem to public attention. Presently, childhood obesity and the health-related consequences of obesity in general are a significant public health concern. As a result, more research dollars are appropriated to find ways to fight and stop this devastating problem. Public health programs can be very effective at illuminating threats to community health and promoting thoughtful intervention.

The recent rise of publications about self-injury in scientific journals suggests that self-harm is a problem that researchers are taking very seriously. Undoubtedly, it is soon to be a pressing public health concern. As research about self-harm accumulates, and our understanding of the extent and consequences of these behaviors grows, public health programs will become more active in spreading information about self-harm. Public health programs work in a variety of ways. The main goal of a public health program is to spread information about threats to community health. This is accomplished by placing public health announcements on television or on the radio, training mental health professionals how to identify people who self-harm, and making services available to those who cannot afford mental health care. One way attention has been drawn to self-harm is by making March 1 Self-Harm Awareness Day. All across the country, in various community settings, people hold meetings to bring attention to the growing problem of self-harm. However, public health programs can be very costly. Funds come from public monies generally raised by taxes and private charitable donations from interested parties. Determining what threat to health receives money often depends upon the result of a cost-benefit analysis. If the cost of the behavior is growing and exceeds the funds needed to prevent it, it is more likely to receive money. There is a lot of competition for both public and private dollars. Researchers and public health workers must work hard to convince others that self-harm is a serious, growing problem that requires immediate attention.

RESEARCH UPDATE

The scientific study of self-harming behaviors is just beginning. There are still many questions to answer about these behaviors and who engages in them. However, there are several obstacles to studying self-harm. One such obstacle is that many self-injurers do not want to be identified. People who practice self-harm are often very good at hiding their behaviors. As a result, it can be very challenging to identify those who need help. Additionally, many people who self-injure are reluctant to give up their self-harming behaviors. Like someone with a drug or alcohol problem, a person who self-injures often believes that self-injury makes their life more tolerable and cannot imagine life without it. Thus, awareness of self-harm must be made a priority. If people keep talking about the problem, those who engage in these behaviors might be more likely to see them as a problem.

Another obstacle to studying self-harm is that there is very little consistent information about the behaviors and, as such, no shared vocabulary about the problem. Self-harm is also called self-injury, parasuicide, self-mutilation, self-abuse, and cutting. The lack of consistent terminology can prevent effective scientific communication. Much of the ambiguity about self-harm emerges from the fact that self-harm is not recognized as a mental disorder, but rather is considered a symptom of other disorders. As a result, much of the information about self-harm comes from people who have other disorders. In fact, the theory and treatment of self-harm has grown from a more substantial literature investigating self-harm in borderline personality disorder. Without its own diagnostic category, self-harm can be overlooked by clinicians. A patient who lacks symptoms of psychosis, a developmental disorder, or a personality disorder will likely not be asked about experience with self-harm. Finally, a practical problem emerges when someone who practices self-harm cannot receive appropriate treatment because their behavior does not fall under the reimbursement guidelines of a health insurance company. At the same time, without more research investigating self-harm, it will remain in limbo as a diagnosis.

The field of self-harm is wide open for a new generation of researchers. The most basic and essential information about self-injury, such as how common it is, remains a mystery. Indeed, prevalence estimates are varied and as such clinicians and researchers remain uncertain about how much of a threat self-harm poses to each community. Although self-harm appears to be on the rise, the reason for the increase is unclear. Additionally, there is no reliable portrait of a typical self-harmer. There are many theories about why people practice self-harm but very little supportive scientific evidence. Thus far, medication treatment is in its experimental stages and has been shown to have limited efficacy. Psychological treatment programs are mostly limited to patients with borderline personality disorder or those who can afford costly and time-intensive psychodynamic psychotherapy. New and more streamlined treatment methods designed to help eradicate self-harm are essential to ending this dangerous behavior. A young person interested in beginning a career in the mental health field would have much to contribute to a new and growing area of clinical work and research.

YOUR TURN: HOW WOULD YOU INCREASE AWARENESS ABOUT SELF-HARM?

Perhaps after reading this book about self-harm you have more questions than answers. What information about self-harm would you like to know? What kind of a study would you be interested in conducting? How would you go about convincing a funding agency to fund your study? With whom would you choose to share your results: an academic journal, school systems, or practitioners in the mental health field?

Do you know people who practice self-harm in your school? Perhaps you believe that more people need to know about the problem of self-harm and join the fight to stop it. If you were asked to design a public health program to inform people about self-harm, how would you go about it? To whom would you like to convey information: students, teachers, parents, or politicians? What channels might you choose for spreading information about self-harm? How might you increase awareness about this phenomenon?

· · · · · · · ·

SUMMARY

Although revealing causes and effective treatment programs for self-harm is important, it is even more essential to find ways to prevent others from beginning the practice. People who work to promote health in a community and prevent medical problems work in the public health field. A public health approach can help spread information about the dangers of self-harm and potentially discourage new people from hurting themselves. Research in the area of self-harm is still very new. There remain several unanswered questions and there is little agreement about how to define and discuss self-harm. The next phase of research in self-harm should focus on clarifying these most basic issues.

NOTES

1. A. R. Favazza and K. Conterio, "The Plight of Chronic Self-Mutilators," *Community Mental Health Journal* 24, no. 1 (Spring 1988): 22–30.

2. J. Briere and E. Gil, "Self-Mutilation in Clinical and General Population Samples: Prevalence, Correlates and Functions," *American Journal of Orthopsychiatry* 68 no.4 (1998), 609–620.

3. S. Ross and N.L. Heath, "Two Models of Adolescent Self-Mutilation," *Suicide & Life-Threatening Behavior* 33, no. 3 (2003), 277-287.

4. J. Radcliffe, "Self-Destructive "Cutters" Live Their Lives on the Edge," *Los Angeles Daily News*, March 28, 2004.

5. P. Boyce, M.A. Oakley-Browne, and S. Hatcher, "The Problem of Deliberate Self-Harm," *Current Opinion in Psychiatry* 14 (2001): 107–11.

6. See note 1 above.

7. See note 3 above.

8. E. Wurtzel, *Prozac Nation* (New York: Riverhead Books, 1995), 46–47.

9. Armando R. Favazza, *Bodies Under Siege: Self-mutilation and Body Modification in Culture and Psychiatry*, 2d ed. (Baltimore: Johns Hopkins University Press, 1996).

10. American Psychiatric Association, *Diagnostic and Statistical Manual of Mental Disorders*, 4th ed, Text Revision (Washington, D.C.: American Psychiatric Publishing, Inc., 2000), 349–51.

11. American Psychiatric Association, *Diagnostic and Statistical Manual of Mental Disorders*, 4th ed., Text Revision (Washington, D.C.: American Psychiatric Publishing, Inc., 2000).

12. Trichotillomania Learning Center, "You Are Not Alone!" http://www.trich.org/about_trich/not_alone.asp (accessed December 11, 2007).

13. See note 11.

14. NARSAD Resarch, *Fact Sheet: Borderline Personality Disorder*, http://www.narsad.org/dc/pdf/facts.bpersonalityd.pdf (accessed December 11, 2007).

15. A. Favazza, L. DeRosear, and K. Conterio, "Self-Mutilation and Eating Disorders," *Suicide and Life Threatening Behavior* 19, no. 4 (1989): 352–61.

16. A. Favazza and K. Conterio, "Female Habitual Self-Mutilators," *Acta Psychiatrica Scandinavica* 79 (1989), 283–89.

17. Amanda Purington and Janis Whitlock, *Self-Injury Fact Sheet*, http://www.actforyouth.net/documents/fACTS_Aug04.pdf (accessed December 11, 2007).

18. A. Favazza, L. DeRosear, and K. Conterio, "Self-Mutilation and Eating Disorders," *Suicide and Life Threatening Behavior* 19, no. 4 (1989): 352–61.

19. J.L. Herman, J.C. Perry, and B.A. van der Kolk, "Childhood Trauma in Borderline Personality Disorder," *American Journal of Psychiatry* 146 (1989): 490–95.

20. K.L. Gratz, "Risk Factors for Repeated Deliberate Self-Harm Among Female College Students: The Role and Interaction of Childhood Maltreatment, Emotional

Inexpressivity, and Affect Intensity/Reactivity," *American Journal of Orthopsychiatry* 76 (2006): 238–50.

21. See note 9.

22. Erin Polk and Miriam Liss, "Psychological Characteristics of Self-Injurious Behavior," *Personality and Individual Differences* 43 (3), 567–77.

23. Todd F. Heatherton and Roy F. Baumeister, "Binge-Eating as an Escape from Self-Awareness," *Psychological Bulletin* 110 (1991): 86–108.

24. B.A. van der Kolk, J.C. Perry, and J.L. Herman, "Childhood Origins of Self-Destructive Behavior," *American Journal of Psychiatry* 148 (1991): 1665–71.

25. M.M. Linehan, *Cognitive-Behavioral Treatment of Borderline Personality Disorder* (New York: The Guilford Press, 1993).

26. K.L. Gratz, "Risk Factors for Repeated Deliberate Self-Harm Among Female College Students: The Role and Interaction of Childhood Maltreatment, Emotional Inexpressivity, and Affect Intensity/Reactivity," *American Journal of Orthopsychiatry* 76 (2006): 238–50.

27. S. Herpertz, H. Sass, and A.R. Favazza, "Impulsivity in Self-Mutilative Behavior: Psychometric and Biological Findings," *Journal of Psychiatric Research* 31 no. 4 (1997): 451–65.

28. G. W. Kraemer, D.E. Schmidt, and M.H. Ebert, "The Behavioral Neurobiology of Self-Injurious Behavior in Rhesus Monkeys: Current concepts and relations to impulsive behavior in humans," *Annals of New York Academy of Sciences* 836 (1997): 12–38.

29. R.H. Dworkin, "Pain Insensitivity in Schizophrenia: A Neglected Phenomenon and Some Implications," *Schizophrenia Bulletin* 20 (1994): 235–48.

30. J.M. Hooley and M.L. Delgado, "Pain Insensitivity in the Relatives of Schizophrenia Patients," *Schizophrenia Research* 47 (2001): 265–73.

31. J.J. Brumberg, *Fasting Girls* (Cambridge, MA: Harvard University Press, 1988).

32. J.L. Whitlock, J.E. Eckenrode, and D. Silverman, "The Epidemiology of Self-Injurious Behavior in a College Population," *Pediatrics* 117, no. 6 (2006).

33. D. Simeon and E. Hollander, *Self-Injurious Behavior: Assessment and Treatment* (Washington, DC: American Psychiatric Press, 2001), 22.

34. John G. Gunderson and Perry D. Hoffman, *Understanding and Treating Borderline Personality Disorder: A Guide for Professionals and Families* (Washington, DC: American Psychiatric Publishing, Inc., 2005).

35. M.M. Linehan, *Cognitive-Behavioral Treatment of Borderline Personality Disorder* (New York: The Guilford Press, 1993).

GLOSSARY

alexithymia—A disorder in which people lack the ability to describe emotional experiences appropriately.

amnesia—Clinically significant memory loss.

anorexia nervosa—A mental disorder characterized by extremely low weight and an obsession with thinness.

antagonist—A type of medication that blocks the flow or activity of a neurotransmitter.

anterior frontal cortex—The front of the brain, mostly responsible for complex thought; injured in Phineas Gage.

antipsychotic medication—Medications used to treat psychotic symptoms and mental disorders like schizophrenia as well as motor tics.

asceticism—Active self-denial in which religious people engage in order to become closer to God.

autistic disorder—A developmental disorder that involves deficits in social, language, perceptual, and motor development.

aversion therapy—Form of therapy in which punishment, or an unpleasant stimulus is used to discourage an undesired behavior.

axon—The part of a neuron, or brain cell, down which the electric current travels.

behavioral therapy—Form of therapy in which desired behaviors are reinforced or rewarded, and undesired behaviors are punished or negatively reinforced.

bingeing—Eating an abnormally large amount of food in a short period of time and feeling out of control while doing so.

borderline personality disorder—A personality disorder characterized by an instability of moods, self-image, and behaviors.

bulimia nervosa—An eating disorder characterized by frequent binge-eating and recurrent inappropriate behavior like vomiting or fasting to prevent weight gain.

cerebrospinal fluid (CSF)—A clear fluid that is found in the space between the skull and the brain, and in the spinal column.

cilice—1. An uncomfortable shirt made of animal hair that was very itchy when worn close to the skin; 2. objects worn close to the skin under clothes intended to inflict pain.

compulsions—Repetitive behaviors that a person feels driven to perform.

coprolalia—A verbal tic, usually a symptom of Tourette's disorder, in which a person utters obscenities uncontrollably.

corporal mortification—An extreme example of self-harm intended to gain spiritual or intellectual cleansing.

cutting—A form of self-harm in which one cuts oneself intentionally, but without suicidal intent.

deliberate self-harm—See *self-harm*.

delusions—False, often bizarre, beliefs that are held with absolute conviction.

dialectical behavior therapy (DBT)—A type of behavioral therapy used in the treatment of patients with borderline personality disorder that focuses on eliminating self-harming behaviors.

disorganized thoughts—Symptoms of schizophrenia in which a patient exhibits thoughts and behavior that are confused and disorganized.

dissociation—A process in which thoughts or memories that cause anxiety are cut off from consciousness.

dissociative identity disorder—Formerly called multiple personality disorder, a condition in which a person has at least two distinct, independent personalities.

dysphoric—Upsetting or negative. Used to describe thoughts or feelings that occur in major depression.

endogenous opioids—Chemicals produced in the body that help relieve pain.

ego-dystonic—A belief or behavior that feels like it is not part of the self.

ego-systonic—A belief or behavior that feels like it is part of the self.

endorphins—Endogenous opioids; chemicals produced in the brain that help relieve pain or deliver pleasant feelings.

evolutionary approach—A scientific approach to human development that assumes that all behavior evolves in order to help one pass one's genes to the next generation.

externalize—To take one's feelings out on people or objects other than one's self.

5-HIAA—The chemical that is left after serotonin is broken down in the brain. Also called the metabolite of serotonin.

gender bias—Making a generalization about behaviors in which they are attributed to a specific gender.

genital modification—The practices of altering the structure of the genitals to change appearance or function.

hairshirt—An uncomfortable shirt made to be worn under one's clothes intended to inflict discomfort. See *cilice*.

hallucinations—False perceptions of things (such as voices or visions) that are not real.

heterogeneous—Great variety.

impulse control—The ability to control one's urges to engage in a particular behavior.

impulse control disorders—Disorders in which people have trouble controlling urges to engage in harmful behaviors such as hair-pulling or gambling.

internalize—Keeping one's feelings to oneself.

metabolites—The chemicals that are present in the body after neurotransmitters are used and broken down. Generally found in the cerebrospinal fluid.

mood-dependent behavior—Behavior that changes according to strong feelings.

mortification of the flesh—The practice of self-harm intended for spiritual or religious growth.

neuron—Brain cell.

neurotransmitter—A chemical messenger of the brain. Neurotransmitters are substances that are passed from one neuron to another and thus affect brain activity.

nonnutritive sucking—A child's sucking on an object, such as a thumb or pacifier, that does not produce food.

nonpurging—Eating disorder symptoms, such as fasting or exercising excessively, that are intended to help one lose weight.

nucleus—The central part of a cell where chromosomes or genetic material is stored.

obsessions—Uncontrollable, intrusive, unreasonable thoughts. A symptom of obsessive-compulsive disorder.

obsessive-compulsive disorder—A disorder characterized by the presence of either obsessions, compulsions, or both.

onychophagia—Chronic nail biting.

opiates—Synthetic (manmade) chemicals that act like opioids in that they produce pleasant feelings like pain relief.

parasuicide—Self-injurious behaviors in which suicidal intent is questionable.

prefrontal cortex—The front part of the brain that is responsible for complex thought and coordination of behavior.

presynaptic terminal—The place at the end of the neuron where the neurotransmitter is released.

psychoanalysis—A type of therapy created by Sigmund Freud that is based on the principle that all symptoms of mental illness originate in the unconscious.

psychotic symptoms—Thoughts or behaviors that indicate a break with reality or demonstrate extreme disorganization in thoughts or behavior. Examples include hallucinations and delusions.

public health—The science and practice of promoting the health of a community through preventative medicine.

punishment—A response intended to decrease the likelihood of repeating a behavior.

purging—A kind of eating disorder symptom intended to compensate for binge eating. Examples include vomiting or taking laxatives.

redemptive suffering—The practice of self-harm, specifically to honor Jesus Christ's suffering, intended for religious cleansing.

reinforcement—A response intended to increase the likelihood that a behavior will occur again.

reuptake—A process by which one neuron releases a neurotransmitter, which then attaches to another neuron. The second neuron then releases the excess neurotransmitter, which is then taken back by neuron.

schizophrenia—A serious mental disorder characterized by psychotic symptoms.

selective serotonin reuptake inhibitor (SSRI)—A class of antidepressant medications that work by blocking the reuptake of serotonin, thus increasing the amount of serotonin that remains in the synapse, or synaptic cleft.

self-abuse—See *self-harm*.

self-flagellation—A medieval practice of whipping oneself with leather strips as a form of self-punishment.

self-harm—The practice of injuring oneself intentionally, but without suicidal intent.

self-injury—See *self-harm*.

self-mutilation—The practice of cutting, burning, or deeply scratching oneself intentionally.

self-stimulation—A symptom of autistic disorder in which a patient engages in repetitive behaviors such as rocking back and forth or spinning.

serotonin—A neurotransmitter that is involved in emotions; has been implicated in self-harming behaviors.

social contagion—The phenomenon of behaviors being spread throughout a group of people.

stereotypic self-injurious behaviors—A symptom of autistic and Tourette's disorder involving repetitive behaviors that can cause self-harm, like head banging or hitting oneself. Also called stereotypies.

synapse—The space between two neurons where neurotransmitter exchange takes place. Also known as the synaptic cleft.

Tourette's disorder—A disorder characterized by physical and vocal tics.

transference—The unconscious redirection of feelings from one person to another.

trichotillomania—An impulse control disorder in which one repeatedly pulls out one's hair.

unconscious mind—According to Freud, the reservoir where thoughts, feelings, and memories exist but remain out of immediate awareness.

vesicles—Small sacs in which neurotransmitters are transported.

FURTHER RESOURCES

Books

Carlson, M. *Blade Silver: Color Me Scarred*. Colorado Springs, Colo.: Think Press, 2005.

Garland, Jane E. *Depression Is the Pits, but I'm Getting Better: A Guide for Adolescents*. Washington, D.C.: Magination Press, 1997.

Patterson, Anna. *Running on Empty: A Novel about Eating Disorders for Teenage Girls*. London: Paul Chapman Educational Publishing, 2002.

Raskin, Rachel. *Feeling Better: A Kid's Book about Therapy*. Washington, D.C.: Magination Press, 2005.

Sones, Sonya. *Stop Pretending: What Happened When My Big Sister Went Crazy*. New York: HarperCollins, 2001.

Articles

Barnes, R. "Women and self-injury." *International Journal of Women's Studies* 8, no. 5 (1985): 465–75.

Deiter, P.J., S.S. Nicholls, and L.A. Pearlman. "Self-Injury and Self Capacities: Assisting an Individual in Crisis." *Journal of Clinical Psychology* 56, no. 9 (2000): 1173–91.

Favaro, A., and P. Santonastaso. "Impulsive and Compulsive Self-Injurious Behavior in Bulimia Nervosa: Prevalence and Psychological Correlates." *Journal of Nervous and Mental Disease* 186, no. 3 (1998): 157–65.

Favazza, A., and R.J. Rosenthal. "Diagnostic Issues in Self-Mutilation." *Hospital & Community Psychiatry* 44 no. 2 (1993), 134–40.

Herpertz, S., S.M. Steinmeyer, D. Marx, A. Oidtmann, and H. Sass. "The Significance of Aggression and Impulsivity for Self-Mutilative Behavior." *Pharmacopsychiatry* 28, Suppl. 2 (1995): 64–72.

Kemperman, I., M. Russ, and E.N. Shearin. "Self-Injurious Behavior and Mood Regulation in Borderline Patients." *Journal of Personality Disorders* 11(1997): 146–57.

Mann, J.J. "Neurobiology of Suicidal Behavior." *Nature Reviews: Neuroscience* 4 (2003): 819–28.

Simeon, D., B. Stanley, A. Frances, J.J. Mann, R. Winchel, and M. Stanley. "Self-Mutilation in Personality Disorders: Psychological and Biological Correlates." *American Journal of Psychiatry* 149, no. 2 (1992): 221–26.

van der Kolk, B.A., J.C. Perry, and J.L. Herman. "Childhood Origins of Self-Destructive Behavior." *American Journal of Psychiatry* 148 (1991): 1665–71.

Villalba, R., and C. Harrington. "Repetitive Self-Injurious Behaviors: The Emerging Potential of Psychotropic Intervention." *Psychiatric Times* 2 (2003): http://www.psychiatrictimes.com/showArticle.jhtml?articleID =175802309.

Zlotnick, C., J.I. Mattia, and M. Zimmerman. "The Relationship Between Posttraumatic Stress Disorder, Childhood Trauma, and Alexithymia in an Outpatient Sample." *Journal of Traumatic Stress,* 14 (2001): 177–88.

Web Sites

Borderline Personality Disorder Resource Center

http://www.bpdresourcecenter.org

Cornell Research Program on Self-Injurious Behavior in Adolescents and Young Adults

http://www.crpsib.com

Laboratory for Adolescent Science at Vassar College

http://www.theteenbrain.com

Mental Health America (formerly National Mental Health Association)

http://www.nmha.org

NARSAD: The Mental Health Research Organization

http://www.narsad.org

National Alliance for the Mentally Ill

http://www.nami.org

National Institute of Mental Health

http://www.nimh.nih.gov

Neuroscience for Kids

http://staff.washington.edu/chudler/neurok.html

S.A.F.E. Alternatives: Self-Abuse Finally Ends

http://www.selfinjury.com

Self-Injury and Teens (Focus Adolescent Services)

http://www.focusas.com/SelfInjury.html

Young People and Self-Harm

http://www.selfharm.org.uk

ABOUT THE AUTHOR

Heather Barnett Veague received her B.A. from the University of California, Los Angeles and her Ph.D. from Harvard University in 2004. She is the author of several journal articles about mental illness and two other books in this *Psychological Disorders* series. She is currently the Director of Clinical Research in the Laboratory for Adolescent Studies at Vassar College. Dr. Veague lives in Massachusetts with her husband and children.